# Chem Trails
(Collected Poems: 2008—2014)

## Quinten Collier

All rights reserved. This book may not be reproduced or transmitted in any form whatsoever without permission in writing from the author.

Design & Editing:
Bob Makela

Art:
Aaron Makela

Photography:
Laurel Carpenter

ISBN-13: 978-0692541166
ISBN-10: 0692541160
Manufactured in the United States of America
First Edition

To order this book or to contact the publisher go to:

www.BobtimysticBooks.com

Suggested retail price: **$20.00**

Copyright © 2015 by Quinten Collier

Some of the poems from this collection have appeared in *The Red Pill, Plastic Water, Mad Swirl, Opium Poetry 2.0, The Telluride Daily Planet, Automatics, The Mountain Gazette, The Stray Cat* and *The Delinquent*.

# Table of Contents

### **The Mind a Fractured Circus** (2008)
Living Fictitiously..................................................................12
To American History.............................................................15
Blues of the 10,000 Things (In Boston)................................19
Knox County Jail Rag...........................................................25
Mushrooms on Love..............................................................29
The Spontaneous Apocrypha: DeBasement..........................34
The Spontaneous Apocrypha: Notes from the Civilians' War....37
A Devastating History of Sundry Beatific Symptoms...........43
Fascists, Fanatics & Escapists...............................................48
Going Nowhere (A Middle Class Blues)..............................56
Halloween, Oct. 31, 2010......................................................63

### **Visions, Asylums & Encomium Paintings** (2008)
The Dragonfly Guest.............................................................71
The Brave..............................................................................72
We Will Find No Answers, We Will Find No Rest...............73
Young Girl Reflected in a Window as a Woman..................74
Quintens................................................................................75
Bus Stop................................................................................78
Twins.....................................................................................79
Danielle.................................................................................80
Note on a Doorstep...............................................................81
Ullalume................................................................................82
Jerry's Garage.......................................................................83

Epistle……………………………………………………………84
Moths……………………………………………………………85
A Dove…………………………………………………………86
Mothers…………………………………………………………87
To S. in Charleston……………………………………………88
Variances………………………………………………………89
What Entrances Them…………………………………………91
Haydria…………………………………………………………93
To S. on Her Birthday…………………………………………94
Ether Holiday…………………………………………………95
Sand……………………………………………………………96
The Secretary…………………………………………………97
The Gigolo……………………………………………………98
Vagabond's Oath………………………………………………99
Haiku…………………………………………………………100
Nobody, Texas………………………………………………101
Movie's End…………………………………………………103
The Party……………………………………………………104
Two Platonics………………………………………………106
A Kiss in San Francisco……………………………………107
Spectrum (Smoke)…………………………………………108
Laura…………………………………………………………111
The Flame……………………………………………………112
The Labyrinth of Solitude…………………………………113
Army…………………………………………………………115
Inutil Paisagem………………………………………………116
A Future in Sales……………………………………………117
Acknowledgment……………………………………………118
Moonlight……………………………………………………119
Letter of Sedition……………………………………………120
Portland………………………………………………………121
Phoenix Airport……………………………………………123
Haiku…………………………………………………………125
Belle…………………………………………………………126
The Center……………………………………………………127
Invocation……………………………………………………128
Requiescat……………………………………………………129
Transcription of a Lotus Vine in Memphis………………130

Carry Me Down……………………………………......131
A Brief Prayer……………………………………….133
The Epiphany………………………….....…………134
The Ballad of Anna Nicole Smith……...…………….135
Nurse's Song…………………………………………136
Haiku…………………………………………......…137
Nostopathy………………………………………..…138
To a Master……………………………..…………139
A Religious Trifle………………......…………………141
A Religious Trifle………………......…………………141
For Our Lady, a Nocturne……...…….……………142
OM……………………………………………......…148

## **Out of the Ether** (2008)
A Day in the Dust………………………….....………152
A Pensive Moon Is Glued to the Shatterproof Sky……….153
An Opal Dream…………………………………………154
How to Tone Your Belly & Thicken Your Glutes…………155
The Megalomaniac's Satire…………………………158
Mrs. Brambleberry's Psychotic Niece………………159
Happiness Is King……………………………………160
Clearview Townhouses for Sale………………………161
Easy Millions……………………………………………162
Treat Me to Dinner, Louise………......………………163
Glowering……………………………………………164
Vacancy………………………………………………165
The Man Wearing My Face……………………………166
Various Corporate Hideouts & Headquarters……………167
To Be Is to Belong……………………………………168
They're Peaking………………………………………169
You, Me & All Those Lucky Ladies……………………170
Intrigue Is King………………………………………171
Milkshake Avenue……………………………………172
Three Maudlin Marys & Their Sick Puppy……………173
The Mendicant Daughter……………………………174

Coughing Tulips Saved My Life..................................175
Cleanliness Is Key........................................................176
My Pants Are Following Me........................................177
Eegad, I've Been Nabbed.............................................178
A Thousand Degrees Below Zero................................179
A Thousand Degrees at Zero.......................................180
A Thousand Degrees Until Zero..................................181
Look 'em in the Eye Before You Shoot.......................182
The CIA in Honolulu...................................................183
Steadfast Willy & the Gang.........................................184
Chocolate Merchant Dies Young.................................185
Charlie's Doppelgänger's Doppelgänger......................186
Not One Iota of Remorse.............................................187
The Suitable Advance..................................................188
Your Record Shows....................................................189
Nettle Calsworthy, Loyal Practitioner..........................190
Impossibly Cool & Distant..........................................191
Don't Placate the Dolphins..........................................192
Welcome to My Hallucination.....................................193
Mob Boss Devours 3-Ton Meatball, Makes Peace with Local Cops...195
Tender as a Thorn........................................................196
Shrimp Boats Bring Home the Bacon.........................197
No, I Don't Want to Meet Your Boyfriend..................198
Chinatown Memoirs....................................................199
Slick Gus & His Cranky Aunt.....................................200
The Foibles of Modern Architecture...........................201
Thirty Years Till Birth.................................................202
The Berlin Wall Is Alive & Well & Living in Paris.......203
Thanks for the Calculator............................................204
Brazen Simpletons.......................................................205
Don't Let Me Catch Your Mom Smiling at Me..........206
A Version of the Future Annexed................................208
An End Without Ending..............................................209
Ending Without an End...............................................210
An Ending Without End..............................................211

## Chem Trails (2014)

- Pre ............................................................. 214
- Pep Rally ................................................... 215
- T .................................................................. 216
- Capsule ...................................................... 217
- Admiralty .................................................. 218
- Postpartum Postmortem .......................... 219
- !!!Quinten Collier!!! ................................. 220
- Vengeance of the Dream World: .............. 221
- No One's Ark ............................................. 222
- Barges ........................................................ 223
- AirCysts ..................................................... 224
- El Topo II ................................................... 226
- Noah's Ark ................................................. 228
- Sade ............................................................ 229
- AfterWork .................................................. 230
- Infra-Dada Manifesto ................................ 231
- Leper Friends ............................................. 233
- Civilianized ............................................... 235
- College ....................................................... 236
- Growing Up in a Deodorant Factory with a Pen Pal in Tokyo ........ 237
- Mario Santiago .......................................... 238
- Ulysses (for Travis Flynn) ........................ 239
- Popsicle Aquifer ........................................ 240
- Fukushima .................................................. 241
- Don Juan in Hell ....................................... 242
- Marilyn Manson ......................................... 244
- Leonard Cohen, Spy .................................. 245
- Amortization Ampere-Hour ...................... 246
- Ammonia .................................................... 247
- The Beetle Leg .......................................... 248
- Manifesto of the Youth Brigade ............... 250
- Other Green Stars ...................................... 251
- Gravity Lane .............................................. 254
- Woody Allen ............................................. 260
- Occupations of the Elite ........................... 261
- The Anti-Teatre ......................................... 263
- Self-Sacrifice Superslut ............................ 264

Nazi Literature in the Americas...............................................265
The USO..........................................................................266
Terrorists.........................................................................268
Industrial Catacombs, Sacred Hardware............................269
Side Effects Include Preclusive Side Effects......................270
Cher................................................................................271
The DA/The Criminalization of Reality............................272
Death Trip 2015..............................................................273
Don't Talk to Yourself, You're Writing..............................275
Twila With an Oxygen Tank.............................................277
Burroughs' Last Dream....................................................278
Twila Revisited................................................................281
The Cold War..................................................................282

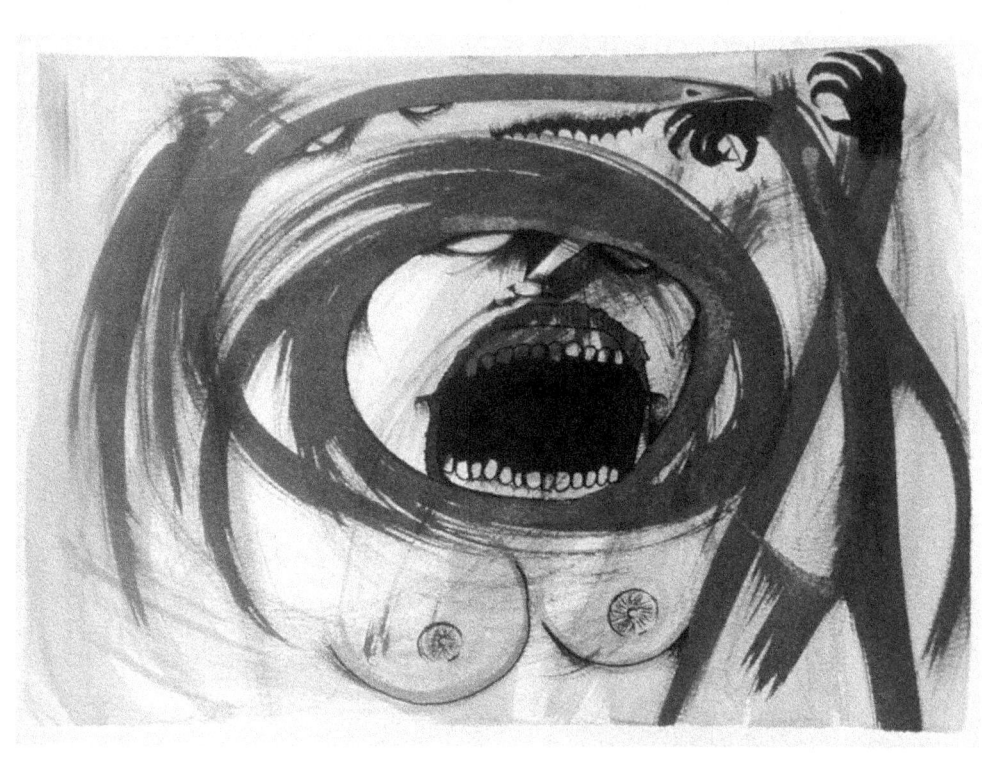

# The Mind a Fractured Circus

*Any overt action against the power structure is doomed to failure because of the techniques of control that have been developed, but the anarchistic impulses of art cannot be governed.*

~Robert Anton Wilson

## **Living Fictitiously**

### I

The outstretched hand of the savior
        Portends destruction:

    There's no escape from his temples
Or the utterance of his omens:

    Commiserate decay confirms justice.

The radio singer's trite lyrics:
        Euphemism.
The poet's unrefined skepticism:
      Self-deprecating analogies
        Defined by vanity.

Personal demise confers humble surrender.

    What if these messiahs—
        Impersonal deities
        Infallible as scholars—
    Falter, abandoning us
    To the dominance of their hopes
    To feign courage and acceptance?

Behind the theatre curtain
Actors imagine the audience
Dissecting the scenes
Like studious disciples     of an undead theology.

    What now that the messiahs have failed?
        Will they perish?
        Are we to attempt,
    Through the turbulence of our wars,
    The immensity of our sacrifices,
    The eminence of our palaces,
            Their reincarnations?

Are we to abide in a silence resplendent with joy
Or fey in discontent
Until their resurrections?

    Does the shadow impart the man?
        The future betray the past?

## II

    A New England kitchen
Contains within its pious limitations
An American maid or mother or,
    As foster parent,
    A bible that changes gender,
Lamenting to its orphans:
      *For Christ's sake!*
*Even the nails are at attention!*

The purpose of Freedom is to play unaware.
The purpose of Existence
Is to play ourselves.

The Absurdist's daily production:
Tiny dictators eat only radio serials for breakfast.
The Revolution
Is a caricature of each living individual
    Dissolved by an airwave.

Attempts to close in on a subject soon spread out:
        Subcontracting HIV,
    Grafting Syphilis on to a diode.

Please allow one last introduction:
    A New England father,
  The television commercials
Forgot to take their meds:
        They're Schizophrenic:
    They've turned
Into dreams.

All is stagnant,
                        On the verge of penalty:
            The species is denied.

                I'm embarrassed
                But I must advertise.

The News reaches for Liberty
Through a policeman's dystrophy.
            Old family and friends.

            Celibate nerves. Acute.
                Smoke at a funeral.
            The stars fall onto the screen.
The view in the atrocity plays,
            Falls onto the screen,
                Proliferates.

            All ideals safe and professed,
                Measured critiques,
                Inaudible persuasion,
                The hands furtive,
*Nothing must ever be dissuaded.*

            The mosquitoes are hatching;
The jungle rides on the back of a hound,
Ripening the tick's naked tongue: The Feast.
                For labor, for our children,
                This is the final discount,
                Helpless against itself.

All forms of voyeurism in a geriatric heart,
                  All rituals dispensed,
                To live
                To see
                The face smother
                The pillow.

        *All we want is to invent history.*

## To American History

I

Clone wars. Zombie wars. Shadow wars.
No exit.

II

    Forrest fire:
    Still looks great.
    Hurricane:
    On the way.
    War for water:
    Gasoline.
    Another murder:
    Wire feed.
    The levees break
    And all the homeless
    Swarm the bank.

III

    You are not my master.
    You make factories out of children.
        I saw the DVD—
            Your secret combinations—
                Not even pennies....
    No one votes.
We see the plan:
    Juvenile prisons,
        Indentured immigrants,
           Pedagogy of abortion and divorce;
The cycles of Being replaced by interstate hotels
           Hovering like comas,
                The stripmall a pastel holocaust,
    The imagination artificially inseminated
                    In the muscle theater,
    Papal casinos blasted in the womb

            Reborn in noxious splendor,
                    Methland billboards,
                Used suicide poems, their salesmen,
Eternity in the trailerpark
            Supercharged and dangling
In the website patois,
                The king of child molesters
            A high school mother,
                    Museum:
            Klonopin,
                    Tramadol,
            Xanax,
                    Valium,
            Oxycontin;
Averagemarriagesitcomcouples:
                            At least three—
            Convenience multiplex,
Fifty-miles-to-the-gallon minimum sentence,
                    Psychiatric barracoons,
            Mechanically segmented strips of grass,
                Propheteers,
                        Genocide executives,
                Third world cosmetic satellites,
                        Statute of imitations.

        Honor is a word the newspaper masticated
                Then forgot to feed to its young.

To the Rare, the Virulent, the Fearless:
                Your sisters are thirsty:
                        Drink them.
                Your brothers are hungry:
                        Eat them.

                    *Fighting Freedom Without Freedom:*
            The story of the governor's dog
                        Smashed with bricks,
                Dragged by its anus,

                    Slashed open with babies inside.
          Now we are secure from sweatshops,
              From our lover's arms
              Beneath the western cascade.

                    Bush, Nixon, Obama, Reagan, de Rothschild,
Medici,
                    bin Laden, Hussein, Caesar, Khan, Perón,
Mao,
                    Castro, Mussolini, Diaz, Bonaparte, Stalin,
Yeltsin,
                    Putin, Pinochet, Thatcher, Blair, Idi Amin,
Netanyahu,

                         Hitler was a Jew.
                         He belonged to G-d's Chosen People.

              Little Gazas, Big Gazas.

              Stillborn dreams sustain the world.

              Earthquake.
              Tidal wave.
              Grandmother.
              Incinerate.
              Out of pocket.

          The sound is always bursting.

                    The rust of a billion ghosts
              Contorted into a metallic curse,
Screeching, the echo arrives before the word,
                    Clinging to the flesh
                    In a chlorine frost,
              Howls corrupted into white bloodless
                         Pristine.
                    The scabs are walking out,
              Sour veins of substitute toenails

> Split until all that remains
> Is an hors d'oeuvre:
> The penthouse in Nagasaki
Where James Bond sodomized himself.

> Our bungalow.
> Our suite.

> Screaming the names of Clara Lemlich,
>         Alice Herz,
> Andrea Dorea.

Even the Earth has her drills,
Cracking the old bones and spilling the petrol
> So we can make ourselves
>         Plastic                    kennels.

> Without shadows the sun lies ahead
In a land where everything is beyond resplendence
> And burning.
>         Take shelter in the names:
>         The gate is locked.

### IV

> America,
>         Go die for yourself.

>         Are you ashamed of your soldiers?
>         Is that why you refuse to feed them?

> Why is it that your convicts are always
So poor?

> Did I reach the wrong extension?

## Blues of the 10,000 Things (In Boston)

!!!!!!!!!     I WANNA HONKY TONK YOUR BODY BABY
!!!!!!!!!

    (It's cold out
        But nobody seems to mind,
        Above, where pigeons nest,
        A window cracks
& bricks dislodge themselves from the tenement).

      Society is collapsible,
Like a cheap plastic picnic table,
        Its hinges are inflexible,
You've got the receipt,
      The fine print reads:
NONREFUNDABLE.

      Ah, the Esplanade,
    Viewed from behind brownstones,
        In a parking lot where my car's not parked—
      I walked—
    Didn't cross the street
        & here my bones are propped,
      Trying not to get hit
Or hold up traffic,
      Here my bones lean
      Against a towering
    Mass of faceless bricks,
      Scrawling songs
    Devoid of music
        (I can't sing).
      Students pass:
Pay no heed.

    I want to see you in lieu of eyes sweet darling,
Bright autumn leaves cresting the green moss of your irises.

i got no phone
        traveling alone to meet nobody
        everybody's got a hat over their face
        but their head's uncovered
        & the breeze, little by little,
        even the fool knows is getting bitter

Using the quarter phone on Beacon St.
The aristocracy instantly declaim and declassify you
        To a folder without a number.

                          TV for dinner—
                        Toothsome delicacy—
                  You're lucky to've discovered
                    I had nothing to say
                    Before I made to speak.

I desire,
        At this particular juncture,
        To unwind on a bench by the river
        Before any of my singular fates arrive
        Like a lady awaiting her dates
In the red light district of the mind.

                !!!!!!!!!    PRAISE BE TO THE RAMP
!!!!!!!!!
        Oh concrete archway overpassing cars
        To my sanctuary.
        (It's freezing out & I'm hungry—
                No cause to worry,
                I'll soon be home
                With a warm
                Woman to feed me.)

    Charles, Patriarch of Opaque Currents,
        Small white sails emerge on the tips
Of your wind wrought ripples,
                Fluttering like zealous birds,

Going down stream for now
      But soon I'll be heading back
To the mountains surrounding
      Grand Junction, CO,
If only in my sleep,
      Exhausted from so much meandering
In words and on my feet.
      I feel the tumble weeds
Flicker down the movie sets
      Of my heart,
Diving off the sandstone cliffs
      Into the sun.

(Oh god, not that Gift of Sadness jive again,
      Maybe I
should see a Dr.
  Or prescribe my own  medicine).

      I sense the ballpoint of my pen
  Rolling in my fingertips,
    That's how personal this wind chill is,
  Seeping into these words
    With a frosty knife blade glint to its fancy.

You found the Tao but couldn't read it.
You had a vision but couldn't see it.

     *Oh sweet Manna*
     *Of your cherry pie!*
   *Said, Oh sweet Nanna*
   *Give me your cherry pie!*
     *As a testament to this love*
     *Increate and denied—*

Was your outfit a success?
  Life is only meaningful
To those who regard themselves by their dress.

          Where you goin'?
*Ain't nowhere more important!*
          Ain't nowhere you're goin'
*But it's still more important!*
You got bad posture,
              Waiting in line without a ticket.

             These limp fashion boys of Boston
Lack any *machismo*.
        They primp for hours
To look like they didn't primp at all.

(Though if I thought myself
A genuine thug
I would be exceedingly more deluded
Than the combination of all of them
Who comb their hair to look messy).

A fellow stroller told me to take things in stride:
I apologized when I took his & made off quick
Like I was chasing a bus with it.

        You suffer at your leisure
             For the taste of a nectarine.
        You suffer at your leisure:
             Even your viruses are sanitary.

          Darling of Vacuity,
I'm sure no placid love song
        Any longer can cause the butterflies in your chest
               To flutter with my name
      Or make your hands tremble to grasp my back
         Though I languish on your bed
Just across this tiny room
        Appraising the willows of gloom
Through the opalescent light of memory.

*Ol' Pot Belly gots his enigmatic brew!*

*It seethes & steams calling after you!*
*An abstract taste fills your mouth when you chew—*
*Just a dab of skeet from Ol' Pot Belly's stew!*

When locomotives howl
    Till your brain falls to your shoes
    It ain't common babe
    You got the Lucidity Blues

                      Cro-Magnon
              Dumb Anglo-Saxon
              I got news for you, child:
                      We're all from Africa.

      (Thank you
  J. Diamond
  for elaborating.)

              Men are women in this garden.
              They come for each other
      In the dawn              hungover.

In every bus station I encounter the same bellowing Negro,
          His voice a burly train whistle;
A blathering caucasian forcing his bronzed girl to act white;
    Italian cockatiels with Las Vegas plumage,
Shrieking:
          Then there's always the girl who enchants me,
          Lugging a guitar awkwardly,
          Dazedly gazing at the chrome terminal doors
    As if they were stars or newborns
              Opening their mouths for the first time.
          I know if I'd only talk to her
(This time I don't, every time I never do)
                She would, like a gentle courtesy,
          Fall in love with me too.

            The unwittingly elegant Indian mother:

    Some unintelligible nakedness of her intentions
        Makes me want her.
But she must deal with her screeching daughter
      Very firmly, thus never to acknowledge me.
All the better, anyway,
     She's married & I have only 73 cents to my name
   (Not even a cigarette),
       Haven't tasted a morsel all day,
Derangement will soon set in,
     Following exhaustion from malnourishment,
That lingering disdain for all the things
     You had the chance to eat, but refrained.
I hope that someday I'll be full permanently—
        I know it doesn't go that way.
I'll be hungry again and cursing
    My digestion for pounding,
    My mouth for masticating,
    My ears for hearing,
    My hands for touching,
    My mind for thinking of ways
       To avoid exerting energy,
   My eyes for hurting the things they see,
     My soul for relinquishing
        To the 10,000 Things.

## Knox County Jail Rag

the inept have sickness,                                                          so please,
                    molest your health at your leisure:

                    pose your bronzed & gifted Adonis
          atop the gates of the Plague
                while their ragged Prometheus
smears the ivory pillars with his fingerprints—

            a man who's been ruined for your pleasure
        will disdain your Cadillac out of envy,
                he's aware of his jealousy:
              that's where the rage comes from—

      there's no need to worry about the boy
                whose face is a pockmarked putty mask
with eyes unable to articulate any emotion or science,
                                  only starvation—
whose mind is enveloped in the personality
(criminal)
          our laws have imposed on him—

      he gathers his fellow inmates around a plastic chess table
              like a king calling his noblemen to court—
     the wine: deluded juice—
           the crystal goblets: styrofoam cups—
this is a king who must obey his guards' commands:
        that's where the security comes from—
not a tangible equanimity, like an inheritance from the family,
     but a symbolic and otherwise worthless kind,
like a diploma or degree—

            believe me,
      everybody knows the rich have problems,
          they're quite vocal in expressing them
    & have the money to buy an audience—
        they say: "I've seen things—

sure they have
vicariously,
too completely—

they have yet to transcend to the asphodel depths;
to strip themselves of their color, their brilliantine—
to breach the increate spiritual division
between their minds and the men they call wicked,
these men who've depleted themselves
through their addictions
to craze,
so wealth could convince those who possess it
that the world is lush rolling hills christened with purple sunlight
constructed on anything but cages—
imbalance would reign over harmony,
good Christians,
without Judas' chimerical kiss,
there would be no atonement,
no absolution of sins—


!!!!!!!!!    LISTEN    !!!!!!!!!


stop shaking your head!
does anyone know what evil is?

it breaks my heart
to hear any human being's hands hit steel bars,
no matter the motive,
no matter the charge—
we owe those we've imprisoned
our full attention & our tenderness,
for without their failure & their hate
we'd be deprived of mercy
with no one to forgive, not even each other—

—the butterfly hibernates to reenter the world as a worm—

               what about the gaunt violet-eyed boy,
                    balding with scraggily beard,
               twenty-something,
                         voice like ponderous slabs of sandstone?
          his religion is the needle that dreams of him—
                    a stout block wall divides us,
               four foot high,          easily surmountable,
                    a bible rests on top,
                         unites us,                    mocks us:
               God is faceless,
                    the crisp turning of pages—
          compact fiber mattress pounds a metal cot—
               heavy footfalls like blackholes of sound—
          polycarbonate glass compresses the frost into sweat—
          yellow blood stains beneath the rubbered metal steps,
immutable,                              the shape of shoe tread
               —rorschach of crimson motion—
stray dots of paint from the ghost assailant's brush:
               a lingering masterpiece of comas—
     a pantomime of the final danger—
          calamity and horror birthing shapes
                    in a tango, invisible, ghastly, orgiastic—
     certain thrust and irrevocably split veins
               blush the canvas—

convicts: YHWH told Lucifer to speak to Adam's rib—

          the Greek Pantheon burst from the mind penitentiary
                    & in turn enslaved Time.

               despair sanctifies:
          sentimentality disconnects the fanatic
                         from the logic of the present—
               thus it must be subverted.
FIX or NO FIX
          becomes NOW or NOW!!!
               guilt is irremediable,
          so abuse it till you're convinced you love it:

                              Addict's Credo—
when a junky self-destructs they obliterate their world,
           escaping the judgment of its occupants—
                     wounds heal & strength confounds them—
               memories forget themselves,
                     to smother the bereft with love no longer—
love displaces the unfortunate as it does their lover,
                                        giver or receiver—

citizens of The Free White World proclaim:
           "criminals speak to say the opposite:
                their humanity is hollow;
                they ask only to be released into a cell,
           beaten till they're raped,           raped till they bleed,
                they desire only to die from natural violence—"
yet every time this happens a vacancy on the street lingers—
                a dark spot on the crystal eye of dirt—

                the pupils of a young officer,
                breath fermenting into gasoline,
                forefinger skin tobacco stained;
                he married a girl out of pity—
           she apologizes with sexual aberration—
                     he keeps her like a centipede in a jar—
                when the sergeant performed the ceremony
                he handcuffed them together
                then briskly read them their rights—

           what have I seen that I should be condemned for seeing?
     what have you done that I should be condemned to repeat?
                     I ask for the grace to forgive you—
                     I ask for you to forgive yourself
                           for having anyone to forgive—

## **Mushrooms on Love**

    Impossible to explain—

Jumpy faces superimposed over the planets and the stars—
        Superimposed over their eyes: whaddayagot?
                *Whatta you got?*
I got the ability to disappear in the middle of a conversation
                With southern diplomats
        Into a blue room backlit by a blackhole
      That instantaneously reflects the gleam
          From a superhero's charismatic grin.

    !!!!!!!!!    YOU CRAZY FUCK    !!!!!!!!!

      *I* got the capabilities to brandish
A sparsely decorated kitchen table
         & exploding pustules
During my infrequent visits to the surface—

      It occurs at a Dr.'s office—
I'm posing as a pale magazine cover
         Arranged congenially on the corner cabinet,
      Contemplating the lackluster floor tiles
As a dyslexic hag sells her daughter's pristine eyes
         For pennies on the dollar—

A sterile smile phosphorescing
With reluctant concupiscence promised, accepted—

              Polyphony of stereo
   :Organic voices                   :Recorded voices
:Sirens overdubbed to remind us—

    *We're science fiction space cadets*
        *Emerging onto the ashen pink terrain of Hell*
      *From a fold in Eternity—*
Giggling like morons enchanted by mystic incantations—

Previous to our adventure
We'd read scriptures from the Bible backwards

!!!!!!!!!THAT'S
WHY!!!!!!!!!

Impossible to imagine—

Forgive us—

Still horizon—

The polyphony degenerates—
    Cacophony spews from our rocket's tongue—
Jagged orange sharpens into red—
    As our descent quickens,
Emitting a furious jungle rhythm
    Lifted from apocryphal symphonies—
    Those composed in a deft calamity—
    All creatures became androgynous—
Fractured gospels propagating themselves—
    Our plunge accelerates—
    The pace is unbearable—
    The fauna here have no use for tears—
They use their madness to defeat themselves—
    All natural compounds—
    Our machines invented them—
    They developed their *IMAGES* into *US*.

That's my ability:
To disappear into psychic compilations of words and symbols—
    Photographs of familiar places—
    Soothing pictures where galaxies play—

Remember—
    The image begat of words—
The image engendering the virus—

See:
>  The exonerated buffoon take a cement dive—
>    Impossible to ignore—
>      Impossible—

>    The billboard advertisements in Hell—
>    Murderous whispers of an axe in the dark—
>    Joy—
The local carnival propounds any visceral human malfunction—
>            The ringmaster worn by his hat—
>      Opaque flashes of music terrify the spectators—

>    Impossible to halt—

>              !!!!!!!!!   NEXT INSTALLMENT
PLEASE     !!!!!!!!!
>                !!!!!!!!!     IMMEDIATELY
!!!!!!!!!

>            Impossible to explain—

>      Biologically outfitted to annihilate language
>      The spiritual adepts interrogate Lucifer face to face—

*We tied that swollen motherfucker to a Roman pillar*
*Then fileted him with his own dick hair*
>    *Before the majority of history was falsified—*
*We went surfing in stone loincloths with Hawaiian natives—*
>            *Frogs were speaking English—*
>      *Bloated monks from a grinding archipelago*
>            *Shimmered as they danced on the waves—*
>      *Sipping martinis of course—*
>        *Seeking to turn the tide, so to speak—*

>        Impossible to utter—
>            Against itself—
>      It was too minute & brilliant an occurrence
>    To garner the attention of the omniscient media.

*Our company oversees the stock*
*Of communicative devices in Eternity,*
*We guarantee that every subjunctive is treated as an individual*
*When placed alongside other relics from bygone days.*

We had a personal anarchy, like love—
Later we roasted my associate
With an overimposing apple in his mouth—
A mouth that had formerly assigned new definitions
To archaic & mispronounced—
Involuntarily salivating as his flesh bubbled—
His skin charred then flaked—

Impossible to explain—

*That bloated motherfucker Beelzebub will never*
*Shake his head at me AGAIN!!!*

A swift tenor accompanies a sudden pulsing of drums—
Nearly inaudible—
Brought to you via a psychic nowhere
Without structure—
Spare yourself the content—

Your mother's vibrator superimposed over the cosmos—
Bored witch doctors christening with surgical procedures
Ignominious church halls—
Superstitious ghosts perpetuating the future of Nonexistence—
Meet me at any random shindig—
Abandoned nuclear waste plant—
To discuss the depth of your grave—

Footsteps double as they echo,
Bouncing from the sides of fresh rain,
The vinyl walls of pastel homes
—Not mere houses—
Chattering down these corridors & streets,
This domain of concrete,

        Veiled in frail sheets of paint.

I am the one who has yet to be born—
        Born of unspoken words—
    My guise is a verbose moment of gloating—
            I am the villain, the playwright,
      & the audience—
  I am in this world,
      Though the creator of others—
  I pursue, through my extravagant ridicule of fame
    & its stench of imperceptible corpses rotting
  As they jabber over a glass of chardonnay,
                  Infamy—

        Impossible to stop—

## The Spontaneous Apocrypha: DeBasement

At last these recluses in their suits of pride,
Overseeing our academic & religious corporations,
Will be forced to admire the cunning virtues of the youths
Dredged out in the gutters of their ruin.
                With the bombast,
                The deafening gestures,
                Defensive signals,
                Telephone roar,
They'll dispute the moral judgment of any party or any truths—
                        You'll readily shake their hands,
                Increasing your confusion,
                      As they tactfully purport,
                With radiant smiles and seedy gazes
                        To desire your most pleasurable company
                    At a ceremony of official circumstance
            While even the gods who worship these
                        Catastrophic gentlemen
                Cannot break loose.

Emily Dickinson adorned a penny dress
& in a stupor of self-acknowledgement,
        While humbly exhibiting her patient bosom,
Her honeysuckle compost breath,
Confessed her longing for a man
        To stun her womb
Eliciting from her mouth a Hep C sex tape.
        Her sparkling chains are never in disuse,
They guard her against the terrors
        Of frequent bondage & abuse,
            & all these unknowable revelations
                That from the holiest of prophets
                    Cannot break loose.

The neurotic priest's acolytes
        Claim to offer nourishment
        For your sexually depraved soul.

                They'll happily provide hypnotists
                To nurture the divisions & rifts
                    That typically exist
                Between a tyrant & his patriot.
                    The preacher's fall
        Will abbreviate the World Series for us all if we
                                    Cannot break loose.

        The seasons play a vital role
                In the dramatic transitions of scientific records;
                            The planets in their orbits;
                            The jets encircling the planets;
                            The distance to the sun;
                            Predictions that come true;
                            Media sensations;
                Every theory
                        That cannot lead itself:
                        Beat them at random;
                        Entertain no financial interests;
                    Beg to justify your time.
                        Our lords are impoverished in our image,
                Confined to the grip of impregnable falsehoods &
                                    Cannot break loose.

                    Every age comes down to this:
            Trust no one, especially in distress.
                    Every year comes down to this:
        The hideous are equal and the blessed are the blessed,
                    Filthy are the poor
                    & hungry are the rest.
                The power of their dominion—
                        The tribes they turn into Natives—
                The doctors who, from their awful progeny,
                                Cannot break loose.

        With a sniper rifle C.I.A. Mohammed begins the insurrection,
                Petitioning his comrades—
                        As if pleading to the moon for deliverance—

An insomniac's interminable catcall
        Never to return to the Circus:
Neon dolls, cars with lasers
        & a village of shrinking chemo patients
Who sell their piss on eBay.
They swallow diamonds in the torpor,
        Owned by this idea of Forever, they
        Cannot break loose.

The silent flowing regime of night, a deteriorating condor,
    Wonderland's last concert, a lactating corpse—
Grinning children pass out names to their spectral ancestors—
    The Director screeches wildly—
His omnisexual producer declaims a variety of actors—
Faceless Despot the Jester robs the concession stand
    Where our forefathers nationalize idiotic decency in
*The Report on the Forecast of Sonic Fertilization in the Corpulent and Homeless as Regards Economic Possibilities in Developing and Third World Countries Including the Military Implications Drawn from the Inculcation of a Deficit*
    *From Which All Undesirables*
        Cannot Break Loose.

A weary traveler's dissipated ego waltzes into the bar,
    Metabolizing the morning, the AGENDA,
Bursting with kinetic energy,
    Rattling inside his snake-skin boots:
        Forlorn, he picks up his bronze trumpet,
        Blows the angel tones,
    As the rest of the band returns to infancy.
        He is everyone's lover,
            From his timbre we draw our bodies,
    The serpents he escorts in us
        Cannot break loose.

## The Spontaneous Apocrypha: Notes from the Civilians' War

In this role you portray a maniac strung out on perfection,
   A deranged idolater with the intellectual comment,
An uncanny aptitude for misquotation and lithopedion guile,
        Your enemies defame themselves.
        Your every word is a lie.

Dr. Freud required of his lawyer certain depositions,
        Information silhouettes,
    The curtain transparent—
                The portrait arrives at emaciation.
       The Chosen:
           Shop window yoga.
        No more charisma,
              Only exposés:
*Death as the New Hope for Process without Eternity—*
*Liberty as a Concept That Must Be Eradicated to Be Gained—*
   *Hope Against Hope in the Retirement Home—*

Her swimming pool surrounds her,
     A filter against all archetypes:
*The World Is Getting Stoned & Hep—*
   *Nothing Makes More Sense than Nonsense—*
*The Celebrity Fascination—*
   *Here Come the Psychiatrists—*
   Clouds of smoke rising from prior office visits:
      *Failed Hypnosis—*

The sky is dismal.
   The rest of the backdrop has been requisitioned by the police.
They are using the cankerous garages and dog food factory
     As the manger for The Nativity of the Swollen Tooth.
       This gives the Bible tremendous satisfaction.

The citizens are advertisements.
       That is the sole proof we have of our superiority.
   The rest of the world is just gaudy and vicious.

Have you ever watched the news on Univision?

Those people have no idea what a Prototype is—
    Without foreign investment they'd swell up and retract.
        They're made to manufacture,
    Quality regulated, discerned by cultivated morticians,
Purchased on a 90-day trial
    Then abandoned
        In a cockpit.

The oral orchard:
    Sir Isaac Newton under the apple tree,
Recalcitrant as myth,
        Legends on a necktie.

The flower pleads,
    The diamond bleeds,
In accordance with the directives
    Imposed by the sitcom's denial.

        A gaunt Baptist rants from his street corner:
    *Recant the aberrations and bohemian codes!*
        *Cease your petitions to the Messiah!*
*Jesus will always hang on the cross!*

*SQUIRM LIKE THE INFANTS YOU MOLEST!*

    *The Lord will not guest star!*
    *You've raped the bosom of modernity*
  *Then laughed like fatted calves to the slaughter!*
*You're pretentious & balmy with whoremongering!*
    *Malpracticed vermin!*
*You pursue me in alley of my Justice*
*To discuss your personal sanctity & other trivial conditions*
*Of this neglected abortion we call Physical Existence*
    *But when you return to your holes—*
        *HYENAS!*
    *—All to be heard is the disputation & slander*

*Of my teachings & my name!*
*Postal Onanists!*
                    *STD Unionizers!*

Sincere words adorn no vestures of beauty:
          Beautiful words are dissimilar to sincerity?

     Angry Asian strippers & the businessmen they audition
               In the backseats of limousines
     Are dimensionless & suspicious of each other—
     The situation becomes less manageable as the liaisons'
          Take on more and more unnatural commissions.

          Paranoid yet seemingly connected images
     Derived from Aztec mutilations the calendar divined
                         From domestic child starvation
          The year the grain ran out
                    & we all had to go on welfare:
               The voiceless chants.

     The Ten O'clock News:
          *The President of the United States of America*
          *Is just another well-fed heathen*
*Cowering behind his country's incomprehensible organizations.*
*Married to an androgynous mannequin who carries regulations*
                    *From a covert homeland*
                         *Known as The Motherboard.*
          *Russian sand technology is an elliptical desert.*
          *Ibn lawfully arraigned and unlawfully tried.*
     *The Senate is a pervert simulator where aristocrats*
                    *Discreet themselves.*
               *The Holiday Shooter.*
          *Congressman Expense is a simian cartoon*
*Recoiling behind the absence of God & the power of the military:*
                    *Morality remains subjective.*

          A blind vagabond discredits the rain
               As he shimmers.

                    The notions of warmth in the primitive darkness,
                    Praying they won't follow him on his journey
            To higher lands,
                            The invulnerable methods
Made feasible against the artifacts of accumulated reverence
                                                    & hate;
                    Tunnel vision to The Western Lands.

            The garrulous trial of perpetual Egypt
                                    Presents invaluable bargains
            For the cultivated sensualist shop-at-home mother.

    The Anarchist of Infinity still worships, still follies,
                    Inspiration awaited crawls from the edge of words
            Into strife—
                    It all appears in a spectator's dream:
                    The ceaseless scribbles,
            Unendurable lists, the proportion
                            Of vowels to their confederates:
                        A minor poet in his minimized category
                            Compiled from inadequate data,
                    Electronically scrambled monotheists,
                            Impulses that were,
                That age too early,
                            Tampered with and misaligned,
                    Cordoned off by government employees
                            Who strove to be limp
                                Penurious
                        Mockeries of all self-doubt.
                    L'Age D'Or, Act 1: Innocence Absolute:
                        Stricken with the fear that fear is fleeting,
        Nature, like a young mathematician, expostulates
                                Till she sickens herself—
            The bizarre ambiguous surgeons in her diaphragms,
                        Antiquing with needles and centipedes
            Into a spine;
                            The fluids are extracted,
                    Questioned, consumed,

And what is left is a riddle, ceaselessly vibrating.
The newspaper is full of disintegrating eyes
                    The color of smithereens:
They all stare at your name with empty expressions.
        Hack Captain Activist never knew his inhibitions:
His fraud uniform and cheap intuitions refused to cooperate.
            He projects his faults onto transparent paintings—
    The Post-Modern masters vomit in Dutch.
He takes this as a signal to juxtapose a shriek
            Against inanimacy—
                Intimate verge, dissolution,
                    Scarcely adhered together:
The Caribbean palm reader
With the highest priced psychic channel
                    Engenders the penultimate art.

        Now Jung has gone and misplaced his disquisition
            Along with his preparatory notebooks
                In an infomercial.
            Cherry backwater mentalists
    Inaugurate an ovarian root canal for Miss Universe.

            Numberless are the vast quantities of discretion
                Barricading Washington in his garret void
As he shouts into the keyhole through the loudspeaker
                For his press agent:
        *Just remember: Boredom stems from desire,*
            *Ashes taste like exposed fire,*
            *So if you're bored raise your torch*
            *And set the salamander ablaze!*

Potentially fatal prescriptions of sunblock can now be accessed
        So the deaf interpreter & the dumb entrepreneur
            Can discuss the speech of the blisters
                On their ears' tongues.
    Who will be the next to discover
            That glycerin is its own saboteur,
Obliterating local pipelines by accident?

41

The lachrymose reporters riot:

*This is terrific! All the racial slurs,*
*The spasmodic yeast infections!*
*The braying farmers! Donkeys prancing through the den!*
*The ferris wheel still extant!*
*The unorthodox fashionista taking off her legs, diverging,*
*Straddling a giant plaster cigar!*

A delirious eagle-headed snake woman
Arrives from a cacophonous galaxy of shattered neon,
Seized skulls;
The civil authorities, their soldiers, cry in a lysergic screech
She culls from their throats:
The army lieutenants, paralyzed, collapse
In tremors of white hot sound.
The General, commandeering an overbearing grimace,
Frightens away the pedestrians
To deny them the singularity of their Ens,
A goat-headed schemata: *War is no longer play-pretty pretend!*
*We prepare a force then cleanse it!*
*This Motherfucker Earth is a mongrel I don't take a shit for!*
*Censorship is synonymous with scholarship, grandiosity!*
*To the omnipotent stockbroker!*
All the gruesome Nazi grammar pondering its own dead print
Resurfaces in the mistrals of grandmothers
Who write as they minuet
On stray cats and envelopes
In a chaos unabridged,
Never to break loose.

## A Devastating History of Sundry Beatific Symptoms

Reporting live from a feed disclosed in a sewer main:

Lead Story:

A fascist document found itself inside the cabinet of a derelict witch doctor. When confronted by the carbon manifesto, Dr. Caligari paraphrased Dante, exclaiming: *The Inferno of Heaven beckons, revolving above me, courting my gaze with unstrung beauty, yet my eyes still turn to the Earth with fond doting—*

Channel 15,036: All governable citizens are implored to profess any statistical data regarding the situation immediately and without apprehension to the indigenous authorities. We also insist that anyone wishing to remain anonymous desist from calculating medical aberrations. It was Society's sheer negligence that allowed certain classified material to slip into the terrifyingly impressive grasps of foreign regimes and the media is not to blame so call off the two-bit defamation junkies or we'll casually frame a paparazzi caricature of your mother, daughter, or undisclosed lover on the local ten o'clock, awaiting a vast payment through a circuit of phony names and manila envelopes. We're also compelled to demand that anyone who kept discreet relations with the owner of the manuscript publicly declaim their activities before a panel of witty, unbiased corporate councilmen of the Magic Veteran's Kingdom who will weigh your blame in the shadows that crease your cheeks, the severity of your forehead, and the gravitas of your knee caps, deciphering the agitated glints of sweat issuing from your contracted pores robbing you of a potentially masterful declaration of innocence. The confounded spintriloquists representing your appalling case will swallow their own heads then slink away to elders who will confront their noble pupils' neurotic breakdowns with beer sausage and crab nebulas.

Awaiting the tourist bus—
        Awaiting what gradually will come next—

A deflated prosecutor of boredom, after putting the pencil down to inhale some serotonin—the mineral saliva loosening the back of his throat like stale bread in champagne—voids his thoughts to allow the impervious page to continue in its purity before intoning some flattering ministrations to bundled aristocrats who secretly abhor their democracy and covet the throne—

   Awaiting the tourist bus—
    Awaiting what gradually will come next—

A blaze of psychic melodies & translucent fire
     Make me reassume myself:
*I'll think about you when I'm beaming*
   *Then call you when I'm coming down—*
Such ignominious dilemmas have deteriorated
    Into pseudo-psychological experiments:
  We stitch together our mortal threads—
    The fractured bones, the sloughed-off skin—
   Adorn them in the experiences of the dead—
Their eyes doctored with slogans speak with their own tongues,
 Rehearsing procedures forced through microbial interstates
   Until the universe extradites its records
    In the form of a scientist—

It is unequivocally imperative to realize that failure is progress in the opposite direction, similar to a vacation at the office to escape the salubrious routines, insoluble habits, forensic digressions, afforded by a life of pleasure: to abandon the plotted phrases & uncannily sculpted gestures of Mr. Unfathomable, that pretentious man who dissects every island until there's a file for all the shorelines and a hotel banquet erected at every tide change—No danger, just droll lackluster pastel safety goggle aquarium seashell wallpaper room with a view like any other handshakes passing acutely manicured cuticles in a toothy smile from a hallway mirror attended by insincere nods from the bellboy who's queer with feral retracted pupils tracing the mailman's thought stream—He brings a package to invest your destiny with ingenious reinvented seasons name manipulated in the horsejaws of carnal women fleets who were not born in the miraculous fountain of white hot blistering torment—Inexpressible, inescapable notes of vehement surrender from the underground—Implausible ideations incarnate in the ether—Inserted: the bright thorns, the sanguinary tears into the moss-green head of a toy soldier with vicarious needle cigarette then superimposed over the artery of this black and white irreconcilable primordium script, this marijuana born ailment disillusioned, undefined, extrapolated nonetheless without necromancy—The ocean is a character with an impenetrable psyche—We view with detachment the poverty-madness humanity constructs to surround Nature with a psychosomatic drama—The ocean is a sanctuary for mankind's pollution—There's no way out of the petty—The Deep Seed Sower commands you to watch more of yourself to better forget your origins—From the ease of your sedan chair you access the iniquitous stadium—Over the PA the impartial voice of a backwards hero informs you that all sacred covenants are total—The only way out of the labyrinth is through terminal forest flame confusion—With the stammering joviality of a crash symbol Monkey the gravedigger assumes his role as mediator in the dialectical critique without inference or insinuation of anything important so of course his statements aren't catalogued here, though it is common reference that his blood was the molten cyanide spilt to forge the everlasting path to the insoluable construct—Please disregard the lazy nurses; it's possible that their quixotic mink purses will be used as nooses to hang their ministerial husbands—When they feel discarded they behave quite peculiarly—Sometimes they almost acquire the potential to be dishearteningly honest with themselves as well as the anthropomorphologists who study their demon anklet tattoos with photographed consideration for the manner in which they ascend from the out-of-focus mistress embittered by her perfume to a leopard-skin handbag with a face inside it—The desert's desolation is withered away by streams of life and vegetation—Let the dead remain dead, it's their form of living—Mother Cowardice and her parents of unwavering servitude elaborately parade their warning:

!!!!!!!!!   ACHTUNG   !!!!!!!!!
!!!!!!!!!   SIMPLICITY APPROACHING   !!!!!!!!!

He's wearing the mask of Heracles, the intoxicated jibbering frat boy, as he topples towards The Ultimate Destination—In his massive arms he lugs a surfboard and a newly minted editor's copy of The Encyclopedia Apocrypha (available to the consumer next century—) Our hero shouts proverbs into a whore's mouth, becoming an accidental prophet: *Say Me and I'll tell you something! If you put on your velvet eyelashes and your centipede skein, I'll promise under the milky sunshift to soon retaliate for all the convolutions imposed by my digestive tract in the least compelling syntax I can possibly attain*—There's no need to call The Head of Immovable Affairs to prove beyond a doubt that the child older than its ancestor is in reality just some deluded Dilaudid addict projecting his denuded fantasies onto the consumer—The Bailiff suggests: *Meet me at the carnival on an airwave after school*—Familiar Joe teaches his agnostic students to wish to be made vacant so they can fade away without further effort, but there's too much fear in their noise avoidance—Their bodies soon become academic desires sprouting tumescent crowds with wings on their shoulders, sputtering through the garden distilling mortar shells from their assholes onto the prostrate picketline lesbians perfumed with postcard abortion candelabras at the Protestant Republic's headquarters in Baghdad, Wisconsin, where loyalist functionaries study the impersonal coldcase ledgerheads found in innumerable diary margins transcribed by pedomane Catholic comic sketches replete with hallucinated annotations to demonstrate their collective interdigitation—

Cease: All distribution of psychotropic drugs to adolescents; all trials, secret deliberations—Imbeciles analogous with the depth of their idolatrous Nationalist conformity—Gorgeous George stares in no direction with gaunt invisible eyes—The Abyss enfolds him—

!!!!!!!!!   *Get bent Chatterhead*   !!!!!!!!!

*Incite hostility in that bitch Mother*
               *Teresa and that Stalinist Gandhi!*

Self-abasement is divinity—

The ghost embryo of fiction dances on jagged bottles—

Within its feet beats the most unholy rhythm—

Ashes crackle and the bones of a coyote howl beneath the sand—

## **Fascists, Fanatics & Escapists**

Pinwheel gods & idiot savants—
      Chipped steel cogs & fire eating dogs—
Orange-haired feather dusters
      Ridiculing the genuflections of servants—
Agent Provocateur of the Year owns a Malibu salon
      & married the library security guard—
  They recite over dinner from the Dead Sea Scriptures,
    Quoting at length,
Praying as they do to the one who has lived
  Through the end of all things to come—
      He feeds them the names of all his favorite
Fascists, Fanatics & Escapists—

Do not look to the Apparat for answers,
   They know nothing of spontaneous love, rage dismissed,
 Cruelty quelled, the nodes of the generous,
     The aggrieved—
  They cannot spell the sacred words
     That gather on the wind
  As they glaze the earth at snowfall—
 They are unacquainted with elegance, pasteurization, docility,
Shakespeare, profundity, equilibrium, vaccines—
    They have nothing to give;
They cannot offer the widows of Soviet persuasion
      Their services—
  Their certitudes, precisions, rehabilitations,
Grand promotional sanctity gulags, emasculating directives,
    Murals of infected bone & conquered histories dwarf them—
    If they believe they are fighting for Freedom
    Why are they killing mothers & children?
Do they live for the war of love or the love of war?
  Their prodigies of violence reign from thrones of flame
      That suffer as they expire
    To the chagrin of that unholy Trinity,
      That economy of lions turned to pigs:
Fascists, Fanatics & Escapists—

    The nun pimps & penitents
 Squander their meager wages on automated vending machines
Chirruping through the abalone highrise carwash filling stations
    Of this fabular elitist meatmarket—
An impoverished Pentecost of coal-blackened workers
    Spans the tar-frayed highway,
   Destitute, meek & anxiety laden
     As that first exodus from Bethlehem,
 Reciting the language of those around them like children
    Trying to impress their priests,
 Before the strikebreakers and the scabs are called in,
Before the demagogues straddling The Republic,
    Carried on the backs of fleas, the sores on their legs
  Melting in the winter fumes like jewels of blood,
    Their eyes mustard contusions drooling pus,
 Have their way with them, in the name of the gold standard,
     A nation of finks,
    Property enough to rekindle
   All the subdued contingencies of interagency
Fascists, Fanatics & Escapists—

Deadbeat deviants with rosebud spyglasses—
   Transparent mayflies biting their reflections—
 *Everyone is a computer screen*
    Begging for annihilation before ridicule—
      An atmosphere of fruitbats encloses
 The silver dusk of Man's vulgar Eternity—
Beyond the outskirts & the eroding county lines,
    Beyond the waterworks & piles of cannon fodder,
  Beyond indiscriminate perception, beyond Cause & Effect,
Beyond the futon mattress wholesalers of petty competence,
  Slumbers the indefatigable trophy plaque
    Of the beerblathering Brahman hockey team,
 Beneath a newspaper clipping victory map
   —Their faces' heroism photos.
 The air is a film of ashes begging to be imbibed
   By tincan freightliner coolies
     In the throes of cosmopolitan soul robbery

        With their dilapidated chins
Negotiating the purblind interfaces of barren lynx-furred
            Yachting class adulteresses marauding
      Through the absolution hemorrhages
              Their devout undocumented whelps
    Elicit from the puerile stenographers
                  Refusing to record as legitimate
Communiqués from the golf caddy rank-and-filer,
      The Mormon Tabernacle Choir,
   A distinguished Nevadanese coliseum admiral at half-mast;
Legions of corpulent, odious, money-mouthing foster parents;
      The grossly astute, payroll induced,
            The spindly, infiltrated,
Fascists, Fanatics & Escapists—

      You who linger in impotent verdure,
You who have yet to endure the syndromes of Isis,
   Her directionless pyramids,
You who cannot withstand the ivory fugues that populate
      The schisms of her yawning,
   The aliens at her breast,
The tropical rosaries of her thighs' cleft tongue—
May your mouth scream but never manifest a sound,
    Never penetrate the languid colors of her dialect,
        The wash of spirals
     Blemishing the painted lexicon of her afterlife,
The baleful spires encrypted with her hieroglyphs—
    You who cannot sustain Beauty's fog & clairvoyance—
    You who have been sentenced to a flaccid infigurement
Dribbled through a rancid tapestry of public bathroom faucets:
        You are the one we've elected as our Patriot!
To found the fanclub & establish a lecture chair
      In the circuit of pawn & usury!
   Commemorating our most dauntless, dashing, diabolical
Fascists, Fanatics & Escapists—

      Meshach, Shadrach & Abednego,
The dawn in her various stages of habiliment,

    All blowing their noses through the center of your story
About prejudice as if they've contrived methods for suppresing it,
All stricken from this lustral caravansarai
         Of fauns & dung beetles,
  All obsessed with the power of their own mythologies,
  Shamelessly divulging their innermost personal tragedies
    To a new companion for a third time in a banker's week—
      In the mudtoil of future charisma seeds
They engineer their luminous proclamations
        To the inscrutable committee chairman
As they suffocate under the pressure, decomposing:
      *There will be no lilacs in the doorway,*
    *& the chapels on Sunday will stand empty*
  *& the soothsayers like beggars will weep for a salvation*
      *That cannot be had by the righteous,*
    *But let the sanitation cake in the bottom of the toilet*
        *Still turn their piss green!*
     *As it would for any of our post-consumer*
Fascists, Fanatics & Escapists—

    This contaminated zodiac of crisis & creation
Serving as the Doc Holliday to the cosmicomic
        O.K. Corral's Board of Directors
    Erupts into a billion smiling fragments
Then compartmentalizes into a honeycomb in the aftershock—
  Jack Nicklaus, that noblest whiteskin trickpony chauvinist,
    Conjures from a musty patch of pill bottles & leaves
  The volatile apparitions of John Wayne & Charlton Heston
To serenade them with notes that dance like anvils on a train
    *Oh,* he chortles in a toppling contralto: *Oh! I've been*
*Shipping with the shyster*
*In search of riding breeches*
      *That don't constrict my pelvis!*
*In search of mountain perches*
      *To suspend my colostomy bag from!*
    *Passing under a bridge of clouds*
*That sits in the air like the nursing home diapers of*

*Jimmy Carter!*
*Do I enjoy them? Well that Depends*
*On my level of incontinence!*
*The West is crammed with fire,*
*Blizzards interlope through the East,*
*The frozen thunder now draped across the air*
*Like the effervescent gauze of a yeast infection!*
*My heart, like an old sun, has gone nova!*
*It howls as I throw my golf clubs at the ozone*
*Then pucker my sphincter when the nymphs of the fairway*
*Pass by my sand-baked lips*
*As I resign myself to the fate of all*
Fascists, Fanatics & Escapists—

Above, below, behind, before, beside & within us
Spins Mortality's calendar,
      Marked with the blood of war & menstruation;
 Through this myopic stigmata, this caliginous Samsara,
The winter always finds her labyrinths;
    In the cadence of her shadows,
  In the rime lace she spins through the meadows,
        The oaks stand paralyzed & no sentient army may pass—
          FBI informant Brandon Michael Darby
& the Minister of Kulchur Tom Wolfe
     —Who haven't met their quotas in months—
      Are called in to examine some purple grievances
  Adorning a dimension of ivory
       But only after they spend 22 years behind bars
            For courting jackals with harmoniums
   & seducing California turkey vultures with Brutus' lyre—
When they finally attain the pastures of their assignment—
          After a poignantly harrowing internment
    In the Lifetime Movie Channel's three night family-saga
       *Prison & the Fame Industrial Complex—*
     They discover their duties already conducted
& their faces erased from the Gustave Courbet group portrait
    Of the heralded
Fascists, Fanatics & Escapists—

    You must submit yourself to the will
  Of the greed-maddened wagonmaster
    When it's time for school
        & you've put on your velvet evergreen vest
   To prepare for the children of Reality;
It is time to behave amidst the furnaces of the oligarchy
   Behind the airbrushed figurines meticulously dust-covered
     In an advertisement's autobiography—
After all, you're just made of wood & Nature is expendable
& the cafeteria is an infirmary replete
      With centurion pickpockets,
  Rooster-jowled stevedores licking cherry-flavored
3rd generation cigar stubs: *Hey Diddley Dee!*
        *An automaton's life for me!*
The newborn convicts in the nursery trill as they gambol about
     Snatching at the padlocks on their playpens
   Like 1940's factory girls
       Late for their first day of entombment—
Weren't we all just puppets of the clockmaker—
  Pariahs warming our bones by someone else's fire—
When a star fell through the window to shatter on the hearth-
stone
     Bestowing upon us a renewed vision of Life
  After the insomniac's dream of the last 150 years?
   Suddenly we could blink & say words
  Yet all we did was go back to sleep
     As the lipsticked mermaid in her bowl ignited—
The marvels of our humanity were left to be divvied
     Amongst the feverish & illegitimate
Fascists, Fanatics & Escapists—


     Lord Borges grew so accustomed
To operating within the strictures of certain brain frequencies
   He learned to coerce & subvert them at will—
        It happened most naturally,
  Then before the tadpoles dried in the petri dish
     The fish in the tank got telekinesis,
   & it happened most naturally—

In such lyrical simplicity the unutterable form,
               The coloratura behind all personages,
          The wine as one with the grape picker's hand,
     The rhythm of continuum, that satori into blackness
Was revealed & Jorge Luis stood on the threshold—
A doorway from the basement— softly ablaze
          With a transmutation that moved through his skin
     Like the sun dilating the pores of a curtain
Until Juan Perón detonated the scene with his primate jamboree,
     His medieval jongleurs with their tambourines
Accosting Eva in the aquifer of her spiced earthling effluvia—
    *Don't cry for me Argentina!* the dictatrix wept
        As the mirrors of Andrew Lloyd Weber
            Coughed lima bean tofu placentas
Perfumed with turquoise just before Growltiger & Grizabella
          Both dialed the exorcist who arrived promptly
    From his citadel in Waco, Texas
With the executioner's stamp of approval & an attaché of chic,
       Slender racists superimposed against a wasp's wing
   Like a hologram of finely tuned
Fascists, Fanatics & Escapists—

How long did lachrymose Dostoevsky
              Wait in his smog-starched era
   With his subterranean notations,
      His pillories laden with women—
  Including Ann Coulter & her bedtoy Martha Stewart?
   His craven prophecies lurking
In a cellar he expounded before droves
 Of uncouth surly warlocks (Rasputin fan club members?)
Who could read the lines of a tiger like a cryptogram
While imitating the mating call of ostrich-cowled headhunters
        Smuggling in aluminum feedbuckets
  Crawfish basted with fingernail polish
           As unmanned John Deere tractors rumbled
Over the lacquered shrines in their idyllic chiming pathology—
       Tuesdays Pat Robertson showed up
  With his diphtheria closet exposed

     Brandishing the concupiscent scalpel he intended to use
To extract the symbol tumors sprouting like cauliflower
          From the hamstrings of the woman
                    With the fattest ass in the world
    Asquat her indomitable watercooler of fantasy & fear,
Her tongue flashing to the insatiable,
Inaudible applause of her desolate
Fascists, Fanatics & Escapists—

Can you hear the gasp opaque of the ocean collapsing
Into the pure?
The chatter of fastidious television mice
           Wound in the phosphorescent light of certainty
      & its discredited proportions?
On gray afternoons such as this
      Can we sit across from one another
              & pick apart each other's thoughts?
In the hours directly preceding we'll separate to rediscover
   Our nymphomaniac memories longing to caress themselves
                      In public—
   We'll be forced to reconvene, honoring our egos
    To the disappointment of our hamsters—
                    Outside our mouths
   The saliva settles on whatever consummations still persist—
Like renegade realtors in the age of information control,
          Like soft money industrial rapists
In the retail aggregate of elliptical suburban marathon laundering,
     We function as the pariahs of psychic warfare
& your handwriting is not yours,
As we enumerate upon the three great facades, the categories
Into which we all fit:
         You know 'em by heart:
      Sing along with yourself
          (Nobody's listening):
Fascists, Fanatics & Escapists—

## **Going Nowhere (A Middle Class Blues)**

       they want to talk to rain with smoke
         these misers in their gold belts with
      ebony buckles
   ten gallon
               cattle driver
  hats
      they want to acquiesce
to the wishes of their        oil riggery on
  the plains
  under a perishing facade of   locust
    light
   in the mountaintunnels they want their fears to subside
      in a dusk of coal powder
      &
     imported boleros
       for the women who seek them
      will never enter their masculine
       psychosis
         they want to catalogue
           the stars with
  a processor
         for a posterity engineered
   for eugenics
    they want to cultivate prisons &
 home
     security implants name their
    sexless vanities
       *War*

this train ain't going
    anywhere—

brakeman!!!
    Brahmin!!!!
   the sky is coagulating into glass
   & i'm supposed to ask

                    if you care

                        here is a hand that
                                will never float over the
                        kitchen table again
            a choir sucked back            into the stereo
                        an implosion of fruit flies
                            to compose an exegesis
                        on the compost heap

    mother, let me back in!!! I'VE CHANGED!!!!!!!!!!!!

        he's swearing he's changed & it's this
miserable   mildewed   rag   weed   eyelash
dapple  in  the  trailer  park  hush  as  the
methheads  sleep  still  western  annihilation
methods  that  slip  through  the heart there the
maudlin  stricken  unloved  of  god
w/her  fifteen-year-old  picture  everyone's  left
their  breath  on  so  says  the  officer  at  the  door
he's  changed  I  tell  you  he's  changed

                    you have to please the neighbors
                & we're all divorced
                    at the barbeque
                    in our company tshirts
                w/the composite sodas of flaccid eternity
                        to embrace
                    loosen your belt
                    at night in the lawnmower plasma drone
                            subdued in the way
                    there is nothing to understand

                give me justice
                    or atleast
                fatty human melodrama
                    to sedate me
                        give me a naval aircraft carrier

                that is about to sink but
                                can't
                                        quite
                                                co
        mmit
                    give me the nuclear submarine that is ab
                        out to fire torpedoes
                                but on second thought
                                        m a y b e
                                we should wait

                        my baby left me
                    for my lawyer
                            i'm so demented by her wedding ring
                        she'd, hanging out at thrushcross grange
                            & I'm stuck out hunting strange
                        my suitcase ain't gonna
                            leave my hand again
                            call me heathcliff
        ugly gypsy looks fifty but he's twenty-four
                                i can't lift myself into the
                                        hot tub with
                                out her
                                    this ain't my real life
                                i'm just vacationing
                                from cosmic unity
                            in this corrupt amalgamate
                                of lacquered excrement
                            & dew

                some people were
                    just born to get ripped
                off    & i don't care to
                        ascertain it

                            now that's nonetheless for ya

        the curtains open themselves

                    the iris of granite
            printed on a translucent gray shawl
                    who should be murmuring to the
                            carpet mites at this hour in search of
            atonement?

    the cat has a urinary tract infection
                he's disqualified
                    the dog has a glass eye
    & toads sleep in caverns several many meters
                    under the topsoil:
    euthanized buddhas in the dolor of bloodless eunuch
                    vacuum palaces

  we're all connected
            what the hell good does it do us?

                    can't sell it
            can't eat it
                    can't tell it what to do

  you get these microscopic illuminations
& they're about as substantial as chewing gum
            & last just as long
    but MARS TOM!!!!
                you get this book
            & it unlocks the universe
    but the rose garden the plum blossom
        the crab apple
                all irreparably cropped
            the elms will go to seed when you have to
    go back to work in the etc. & their regenesis is
                    just a
                            pain in the ass

    the sheriff is a beautiful woman
wielding a vast amorphous prison cell
                to encompass the highway

        like some silicate silhouette
                when sprinting in the sedans of sentience
the a.m. threethirty drunks flee their tremens of haunt &
    vermin-crazed they reel the towers of chrome city
        hallways peeling like paint
          whizcrackbejingling   slashed
    barstools of faustian repose now jarred spiraling
through windows of lilac air in the heat mirage of august
              street lamps & cicada shrills
        sawtooth winged newspaper clippings
           & warrant papers to arrive in your mailbox
    everyday for the rest of this menial
                  gotterdammerung

no mumma
  tain't meh awaidden un dat tring

    in crepuscular
    raiment
  fodder for the starving engines of
              springsummerautumn
    doggerel of magenta
        incision of hours
    long since past she was
        the orange milk vermilion
    of sacrament & sunfall

      the final motel sign

    the cosmogonical orphan

    you clean up nicebut your face is
still planed & creased & discolored fingerstained
as an old roadmap

        it's nothing personal
the planets, the lunar/solar decompositions
      mimesis of atoms,

          the vinegar, the sponge,
                    the oracle in the catacombs,
          the violent, the pacified
                    manifestations of the gag,
                    the nefarious prank
     &              flesh-hewn rhythms of the
                    blackdrum of space
this joke of angelical horror &                    obscenity
          it's nothing personal
                                        & every electorate
                              is devouring itself
                         & friday you will get a raise
then buy a   brand   spanking    new    beer   cooler
                         take the little kitchen cleaner
                                   & kids out
                         on the river
                              confused as to what is love
                         & what is indoctrination


               this train
                    this train
          i ain't even gettin on it
               i ain't
     g    e
               t
     t
          i  n
            ain't no one
                    goin
                    where
                    they
                    think    they

                    ain't no one
                         gettin off

(requiem)
       the dove lands on a telephone pole
       gray against the precise blue fidelity of the sky
       she plays a harp of her own breastbone
       a girl with a blouse of washed sunlight
       stands corroborating soundless farewell
       with another mortal out of vision
       then i am lost in a cul-de-sac on sunday morning
       not worshipping a god

## Halloween, Oct. 31, 2010

      A little late in the fall
      For sun-cured organdy
      The farmer cages his saplings,
      Cottonwoods, I suppose
      I will never finish
      Basho's Narrow Road,
      That particular desk & lamp
I left in New Orleans.

•

Fields & vineyards.
      Copper & verdigris.
      An orb of birds
      Passing from thorns to catalpa,
      To fir
      Then someone lifted the names off the trees
      & let them speak.

•

            What a fine horse,
            Like the one that pissed so near the poet's head.

•

I would never have guessed that this
Is where they hide the children's jail
Despite having in youth
Occupied a cell there.

      Found dog.
      712-
      3318
      (Aug. 28).

- 

    In times like these
    I remember the words of the Wu-Tang:
    Check out my gravel pit.

- 

        Grasshoppers in the brittle tumbleweeds
        Like jesters in dusty yellow riding breeches
        Popping through palaces of delicate dun frost.

- 

    Fuck your man made lagoon.
    It has a very pretty island, though,
    Like a Bob Ross
    Cordoned off with barbed wire.

- 

Most impressionism:
Feuillemorte leaves reflected in a stream
Passed over by a bridge;
I meet the river as
Lawyers & retired cops
On miracle bikes race past
To achievement & immortal expense.

- 

    The Wild West, I know you're dead
    As I can barely smell
    The mulching brook,
    The algae beard dripping from the pipe's mouth.

-

Let the ant colonies at last consume
This jackass with
His whistle, training yet
Another wretched dog
To hunt.
Let him & "Beth" & his pop gun
Fade forever
Into the whispering cattails & tamarisk.

•

Where do these idiots come from?
    Injuring dragonflies
    Who are wiser in their emerald armor
    Than any of these dry-cleaned adulterers in their whirring
    Under Armor.

•

        Fake artist on cellphone
        W/cane,
        Sofa troll ass,
        Silicone nose:

*I'm on the river trail...*

She should buy a new African,
White bitch.

•

The Christian glory of a freshly mowed lawn
    Transplanted to the country.
      I admit the owner & I did exchange waves
& I complimented him on his hump of earth
Crowned by a tiny sparkling bolder.

The next t-shirt I see

Reads: Herd.

•

Ingmar Bergman is my people.

•

Starving artists need to face it:
The Buddha wasn't fat for lack of sustenance—
Look at Francis Ford Coppola,
*Youth Without Youth* was pretty compelling.
*Apocalypse Now*? Duh.
George Lucas after *Star Wars*, though?
*Kagemusha.*

•

The one-armed man
Pauses to watch a beetle with a furry red ass.

The couple in clean white turbans:
A silver-bearded bear
& a melting
Glow worm.

•

The Mexican cop thinks he has one up
On all his brothers in the barrio
Just like the black cop used to think
He'd escaped the Prison Industrial Complex.

•

Finally! A pair of plumbers
On a leisurely Sunday ride
Slandering one of these zeering dreadnought

For his plastic bullet horn ankle-biter yip.

•

The world begs to be captured
Yet ever & anon alludes.

The autumn in her false humility.
Fuck it all: people, places, *Poetry*.

•

Ducks with green heads & geese
With necks like black gartersocks—
What are they waiting for?

•

    Should I confess?
    I've lied in this poem
    & I'm laughing at you.
    Somewhere there is a falsehood
    Superior to Truth.

•

From Edo to Honshu
Your polyester is toxic to the wildlife
In the parts per trillion.

**To All Those Leaving**

If you're going on a journey you must first see to it that every member of your company is properly outfitted. If you're going to meet Death, you must make sure that every member of your party is ready to encounter ALL the faces of Death, particularly those of the living. If one of your companions is not prepared to see in their own visage or in that of one they love the incomparable barbarity, desolation, and resplendence Death provides, do not expose them to these irrevocable visions. Never reveal secrets to an entity who will ignore or betray them, unless it is to benefit the Greater Infinite Knowledge. Your instincts and your experience will guide you to many souls who appear ripe for the venture; only your wisdom will allow you to determine which of these are worthiest. All humans know each other at first glance, yet it takes a lifetime to teach ourselves what we know. Whether you are Society's illusion dissolving in the clouds or Society is your face in the river's mirror, both aspects are ephemeral and distorted. To view Existence and Inexistence with a clear eye, one must be removed entirely from the trappings of both.

Pax Vobiscum

# *Visions, Asylums & Encomium Paintings*

*You have done wisely to invite the night
before the darkness came.*

> ~Edna St. Vincent Millay

## **The Dragonfly Guest**

Invite me into your labyrinth;
      If I belong I will not leave
      And I will never forget
      The Lady Celestina
      Hemmed in atop her parapet
      By dragonfly and tiger guests
      Seeking her favor like thieves
            Seeking a satin weakness.

## **The Brave**

I taught sapphires to emulate women. I dragged Virtue by a fishhook through the reef. I held Taoism in a stalemate. I sponsored parades and surreptitious banquets inside a Spanish guitar. I donated my wife to the beauty pageant of Privacy. I purchased lightning from an agent of germ warfare. I vomited hummingbirds: they pulsed like sunset. I read the mind of energy. I enacted prostitution for stillborns. I corrected fame. I stole water from the liver of Charybdis to revitalize the youth of toxins. I dissected the Night with a golden void. I chartered a police siren. I procured fog from a chain. I smoked a scarecrow. I prosecuted a gutter. I pinned badges on marigolds. I tempted asthma with pornographic corn husks. I perched Autumn on a cobweb. I coiled snakes into bullet shells. I plagiarized a school shooting. I graffitied the feathers of Quetzalcoatl with stars. I constructed matrimony out of fleas. I reopened the past. I found the desert's teeth on my legs. I sent my mistress to Baghdad to collect food stamps for champagne. With a lottery ticket I militarized sadhus, Baptists, and giant squid. I put your name in the encyclopedia then covered your shadow with a condom. I perfected transience. I seduced Melville with a Japanese blossom. I mapped out the democratic consciousness inside a needle. I poured liquid comets into the beginnings of hydrogen. I fastened a nipple onto the nape of a hieroglyph
>and at the end of it all,
>before the last curtain fell,
>I took my final bow
>and I shattered the Rose with a song.

## **We Will Find No Answers, We Will Find No Rest**

because the human word is dead
because the only instrument left to our music is a cobweb
because our lover will not open their door
because Time will not move our hands with its body
because the wheat is charred
because the corn falls like yellow teeth from the stalk
because our vanity is endless
because the shadow of this psalm will not undress
because the skeleton will not feed
because psychology is an impasse
because the diamond disparages the light
because the chrysalis spills its macabre symphony onto the floor
because the echo has known itself
because the streams will not come near us
because of the predators waiting in the immaculate family
because sedition is relegated to bathroom stalls
because your doctrine is immobile
because one star is absent from the topography of twilight
because the muse has escaped
because the doe cannot outpace the arrow
because the fire has surrendered her enigma
because poverty must belong to all
because the petition will go unsigned
because winter laments the children she disfigures
because our saviors have yet to war beside us
because the soul cannot be manufactured
because birth is the origin of tyranny
because the night has come to an end and Ilium has fallen
because we are the conquerors

## **Young Girl Reflected in a Window as a Woman**

In Youth you carry your demure flowers with grace
Through the hazy mountain's autumn:

In age you shun both a cruel and a fond embrace,
Share the mannequin's gaze, startled.

## Quintens

I

Here is the dawn: a pearl, gauze and gingham.
She can never stay long; incandescence
Drapes the Mesa in platinum vapor,
Transient as a gown of lily tongues:
All things young cease in love for an instant.

II

The light of the room
where you first awoke: the light of the room
that wakes all first things:
the noxious mirage of cartoon colors
threading moment to
moment; idiot elves and princesses
infiltrating our
*living* room where part of what wakes still sleeps,
as the day, outside,
uncloaks each atom to its origin;

we rehearse the mute
crystal, mute yet still babbling, blaring
(is the day painting
on the flowers' shawls? how real is her light?)
a mindless trumpet
for all the other geese—violet, pink,
electrode azure,
pathetic mauve and cold, screen-vacant green—
to join in chorus,
permeating Now with the less-than-here.

I apologize,
but Cohen, Nicolai, and Boots I see
no other way out,
for every door in this house leads either
to lunacy or

The Desert, itself just a physical
manifestation
of the Universe's mental illness
(Perfect Sadhana?)
seeming more often locusts than honey,

till the rain strings us
with your stars, Leo and Aquarius,
Capricorn's necklace
of milk the web that entwines our fortunes—
I must remember
this, read the artificial generic
as a joke with eyes
anagogic: all is changeless, a soul
cannot be tainted
or cleansed; all is passing: a soul is healed

or already hurt,
so where, Na, Scrumptious, do we lay the blame?
Karma? DNA?
Cartoons? The dawn reveals that each atom
has no origin,
is neither here nor there (are those bruises
or chocolate palm
prints crossing your ribs like wolf or squirrel
tracks until your heart?).
This valley is an inverted mesa.

III

Yawn: orange diaphanous: dusk-etched cloud-tides.

IV

Close

your

eyes:

a curtain of

fingerprints

V

A part of me
Apart from me;
dreaming your own
ciphers, nested
against my ribs,
despite how I
contort myself,
bed and futon
support only
one acrobat
a night
(yes, I
am well
aware
that this
is what
the next
twenty
years will
comprise).

## **Bus Stop**

Oh I wish I was
The child God chose
To bear witness
To His Bounty;

But I am the one
He called upon
To falter within
His Mercy.

## **Twins**

I

I came by night
for your symbols:
the raven splayed,
the severed emerald;
between folds I exposed myself
like a ghost
fingered by bridal lamps,
searching for furtherance:
the completed vulture,
the last geode:
abyss.

II

I'm sure you've heard about
my infatuation with the abyss.
It's only vanity,
but come,
share it with me,
cleanse the world of yourself,
the window is open,
the belly of your breast exposed,
I offer nothing:
undress.

## **Danielle**

          The painter chooses her colors
Like the dancer chooses her veils:
      It's sometimes those of pluvial umber
In the penumbra where scarves drip
      Cinders of illucid calico
Entwined by the finger's neck
      The harlequin extends
To slather her mirrors black
      With aphid's milk—
Other times it's the classical hues
      Of quietude and reflection
And then it's as fine an inertia as this:
      To live in the transmutation
  Of althea into a whisper:
      The celestial slips into being
  In the way a girl sees
      A flower in the alleyway

And the night is made of simple birds
We can't hear
Singing.

## Note on a Doorstep

She keeps her colored bottles
    In a box like Pandora;
The dawn brings her birds
    So she feeds them sestinas
Then turns them to sand
    With the ink from her fingertips
And they sing for her whatever she pleases
    As a star ends
Then reforms in her teacup;
    She opens, the gate
Disappears for a moment;
    A moth drops its kerchief
Outside her doorstep;
    She sighs, the candle light
A seed in the dusk;
    The streets are all empty,
The rain absorbs the hyacinths;
    The puddles are mirrors
As they think in reflections;
    A clock wipes a crystal
From its face with its hand;
    A sound changes shape
As it departs its body—

    But who will ever know
Her saints in their ministry
    As she turns from the stairs
To enter the tapestry?

    And all the night learns
Is the color of her curtains,
    How the rose drew its last breath
Outside her window.

## **Ullalume**

What strangest of all madrigals
Spreads the rumors of a vibraphone,
The dust born threnody,
Blue guitars from antiquity,
Like blankets of parallel sighs
Thru the wedding bands in the Hydra's eyes
& the tears of a diamond's facet
With the milk of her name
Not her body's fashion?

**Jerry's Garage**

When I say:
        This is the last thing I want to deal with
First thing in the morning, or
                As the dead end of the day
            Offers its only calmative— Poverty—
& I ask myself,
        Is this gradual decline into obscurity
      Really what they call MAKING IT?
There is no place I'd rather be
        Than Jerry's Garage
      Where his seven children
           —All divine tinkerers of sorts—
Oil endlessly the gears of hot rods
      & expertly disemboweled behemoths,
    —skeletal, rachitic cores,
            only good for their parts.
    The hammers clanging, the wrenches and pistons;
               Thumbing through the manuals,
    The grease stained annals of the mechanic
As the stereo aches the sweet tremulous trills of early 70's
dYLAN:
      Steel-ribbed daffodils spring forth
           On hinges of unoiled bronze.
  There is plenty of beer to go round
    In the old barn
  Where Grandpa Hephaestus
      At his unearthly forge
    Tells you again
        How he's worked thirty-seven years
    & in a couple of months
        He plans to retire.

## **Epistle**

*There is no honor amongst thieves.*

That is true,
For a thief is someone who has much but takes more.

I am no thief:
I am poor.

## **Moths**

       Orange-tailed moths
            hovered around our feet
on Chartres Street.
        In time
    your brow, lashes, and nose
         would come to mimic them.

        You said:
            *Cast your swine to the pearls;*
         *Exchange the flaws of the flesh*
               *for the formula that sucks*
        *fermented honey*
          *from the sunset.*
      *Put all your faith*
             *in gold.*

To make me jealous
       you said there was such a thing
   as Virtue.
         It moistens the habits'
        Inflorescence.

        You said:
           *I know the world exists*
              *for our lovemaking*
         *as I know*
            *the insects*
       *in their season*
           *will devour us.*

## **A Dove**

      Who is so brief and vagrant  
           Through infinite grief  
    As a dove?  
       Yet who is more welcome  
                As savior  
  In the voiceless trials  
      Of dawn?

## **Mothers**

The Hispanic mother
Fed her daughter and son
Daisy-colored chocolates
On tortilla chips
Rapt in each tiny miracle
They performed with their chewing.

A girl, who was only an instant ago
A daughter,
Nurses her son in a window
Fashioned from winter
As the pristine light of January
Smooths her long brown hair.
A shadow from the kitchen
Falls across her shoulder;
The cat paws
At the bottom of the door;

Here is the man I was,
Trapped in a house full of mothers
Whose only concern
Was the warmth of their sons.

## To S. in Charleston

There are few sounds
Sadder and more comforting to a man
Than the clinking, sputtering,
Shuffling and tinkling of a woman
Readying the kitchen on Sunday morning.

It is how we first recognized our mothers
And how we will forget our wives.

## **Variances**

  I watch from the other side
    Of the window the world passes by
  And each time she passes she changes her dress,
    Her hair is a different color,
  Her thighs a different width,
    Her figure resembles a number
  And each time she passes
    That number grows more infinite
  Until it ceases to exist;
    Each time she passes
  She carries a new purse,
    Walks a new dog,
  Looks through a new   astrologer
    Who asks for her secret:
  *But first,* she replies,
    *I must keep it*;
  Each time she passes
    Light runs like water through the smoke
  And if she lacks a cigarette
    The light divides
  And she smokes a prism.
    Ravished or austere?
  Is she principled? Celibate? Beyond?
    Each time she passes
  She prepares to become invisible—
    She may wander in and out of the crowd
  But her longing is perfect when she's alone;
    Her skin is never the same tone;
  Her eyes are both liquid and solid like marbles;
    She expands beyond the limits of the flesh
  Then starves in accordance with the plan.
    She is charmed, floating in a lens at dusk;
  She takes off her slip then suddenly
    All the birds are naked;
  There's a waterfall pouring from her hand
    To the gutter;

                    Her ankles are slender;
        Her tiny fingers like white gloves
                    Polished with apricots;
                              She is old and her petticoat is mangy,
                    Her stockings dappled with mud,
                              Her joints creek like rancid sunwheels;
                    She passes by again and the voyeurs' eyes catch fire;
                              Her umbrella collects the ashes;
                    She passes with a broom
                              To sweep the crickets from the alley,
                    Her lips aquiver,
                              Her hands replaced with olive branches,
                    Her eyelashes gathered in citrine;
                              She passes by when lapis streets resonate heat
                    As she does when they are pooled
                              And the night is cool,
                    Evaporating in her teeth;
                              She passes by
                    Unaware that she is asking questions;
                              Without thought she dreams of herself
                    Screaming at incandescence,
                              Staggering, spilling her drink,
                    Then she wears a shawl,
                              A eulogy;
                    She kisses the absence of all;
                              Each time she passes
                    She does not think of herself as passing,
                              She never stops to wonder
          If her passing has begun
                              Or if someday it must end;
                    She never pauses
                              To reflect upon who might replace her
                    Or if she must replace herself;
                              She never enters the room on the other side
                    Of the window
        The world passes by.

## **What Entrances Them**

it is not
the flower
caressing
her ribs
it is not
the vinous
stain on
her lips
how they
blossom
enfold
and wilt
it is not
her nails
cerulean
crimson
or jade
it is not
her bracelets
or anklets
of wind
bright as
the sun
balanced on
her hips
it is not
the feathers
or wings
of her hair
the waterfall
of sequins
pouring from
her breasts
it is not
her arms
or legs

incarnadine
serpents
it is not
the crowd
their brazen
ululations
it is not
the howls
of master
or servant
it is
the veil
that will not
be lifted
in the spiral
arcade
of her dance

## **Haydria**

      Alabaster suffused with flame:
            Mane of breathing russet;
            Rapt; wise; insinuating
            Sunwheels of flesh
            Into the exquisite isolation of Being;
            Time depicting her to herself;
            Her maidenhead in eternity
            Like a magnet pulling into itself;
            She giggles as hummingbirds
            Gestate inside an ear of corn;
            She dispels a moment
            Into the outer reaches of an hourglass;
            She is only real
            When her depictions
            Allow her to be;
            Her reflections,
            Like a consortium of lovers
            Jealous to portray their own identities,
            Cannot look into each other's eyes.
They do not hear
As she dissolves in the slipstream
Where the polarities elope
With the kingdom of Matter
      And all that is concealed
   Is all that is seen.

## **To S. on Her Birthday**

              Light bends
      As it slips in all directions,
Folds in waves;
         The focus splits in the tree limbs,
Opening a prism;
              The rays tangle in your fingers
       Like yellow ribbons
          Or silver strands of hair
     Only the bedroom calls to witness:
Light becomes whatever it touches:
       Divines the future and the past
Before it goes
       Where all things go
That vanish and remain.

## Ether Holiday

                                                                                d

                            e


                                         t

                a


the temperature was the coldest on record     n
mosaics of frost subcutaneously collected
and soon she mistook her skin for the snow   i
until she let herself in
to the winter                                    m
her eyes opalesced
the gnawed silver of her lips                e
parted to exhale                  s
but with the surge of her breath
like down in the wind         s
whirring skyward       i
she                  d

## **Sand**

Citrine chips,
        Grains of salt,
Cloudy white and orange stones
        The size of insect eyes,
Flecks of amber and copper and milky red,
        All mingled with minuscule beads
Of lusterless black coal.

## **The Secretary**

I have an assistant.
        She is very pretty.
        She finds the words to type
                In the ways I obsess her.

## The Gigolo

    I am here to collect
           The textures of your skin
    And it will not be a theft:

    I can fill up your nerves
           With a razorwire circus
    Or if you prefer
           I will trace continents.

    In velour and velvet
           Madrigals of moisture
    I will meticulously conduct
           The currents of your flesh

    And it will not hurt me
           To leave you despoiled,
    Pursued and wretched
           As was your command.

## **Vagabond's Oath**

The lessons of The Whip—
The mandates of The Scriptures—
Nothing compares
To The Wisdom of the Road.

## **Haiku**

        Anyone can be
                anything— Thank you friend, but
    I'd rather un-be.


Why must we be named?
        Clouds, drops of rain, all live
Anonymously.


           Let's visit water!
                Let's atomize our spirits!
           Let's rehearse the fog!

## **Nobody, Texas**

Hazel-eyed Mariah
Has been counting out the register
Since I walked into this cafe
An hour and twenty minutes ago.
She's simple to look at,
Not a princess,
But she has dimples,
And lips that pout
And make you wonder.

Off 2nd and San Jacinto
The dogfaced valet boy
Kneads the palms of his hands
Like a yegg
Anticipating a big score.
It's humid
And the sweat runs down your spine
In rivulets of cafeteria water.
Your throat is raw from cigarettes.
Your neck is knotted from too many nights on the floor.
There are no clocks.

*Two sugars,*
          *Two creams,*
      *Two doors to the street.*

Bald-head Ned dyes his eyebrows
And the few limp hairs
Of a youth
That remains
A remainder.
With marshalled pettiness
He dictates his order
And he hasn't eaten at home
Since Peggy left.

Carmen orders coffee
In her black suit pants
And pajama top.
Her bitterness towards men
Is what drives them away
But it's the only thing
That gets her up in the morning.

*Two sugars,*
              *Two creams,*
        *Two doors to the street.*

## Movie's End

        Don't tell me again
How the movie ends:
        With a sparrow's song
Or the Pharaoh's drum;
        With a bullet that rips
Through the god-hero's lung;
        With a comet that sits
In the sky like a plum;
        I think it would be best
To over-produce your silence;
        If never you claimed
The critiques of the rain,
        And if once you did
Be kind enough to pretend
        Not to foresee
The boots we will lick
        When the film runs out
And our ticket is spent.

## **The Party**

                The dancing violins
           Guide your body in my hands;
                The tarnished songs
                The gold recitals
                Of November
                Turned to bronze
    Still possess us,
    Still the water
    In your mouth
    Cleans your confessions;
            You quench your thirst
                With the thirst of the evidence—
I've seen you quenched,
Besieged and barren:
            New Year's Eve in the desert.

How much of this mirror is yours?

The last thing I recall
    Is a champagne flute
  Extrapolated—

Disavowed—
Subterfuge—
Preforgiven—
    All deserving both life and death
        For identical reasons;
    All bedraggled,
        Coercing their bacchanal
      Into the canyons,
        The corridors through corridors,
    Illiterate floods,
        As I, marked with their number,
      Waste no time
           Beseeching the host.

*Death can come for me whenever she likes,*
*I won't even ask what she's wearing.*

    I would rather,
        Than live forever,
            Translate the cuneiform ringlets of your nipples
                      Into thunder.
    I would prefer to pollute the door to space
        With a garden
        Where a dream can call its fragrance
            By its proper name.

Are you the jailer
        And this is your prison?
Are you an exile
        And this is your freedom?
Are you a sinner
        And this your atonement?
Or are you a sanctuary
        For a fugitive?

    When our affair is over
        Will you let me go back to the party?

## **Two Platonics**

      Light beings dance
           On mercury legs—
      They bend the lens
           Into their bodies
      Their fingers incorporating
           Into the ethyl.

      Midnight is a muslin shroud
           Becoming oblivion
      To mask it:
           An onyx curtain
      Smoldering at the edges
           With fireflies.

## A Kiss in San Francisco

she tastes like lavender

and hyacinths

as they undress

and their old forms of sense

are changed back into earth

## **Spectrum (Smoke)**

                        She's just over there in her mind,
                                  Being,
                               Like Kali
Rehearsing Time,

                      Practicing her web
                            Till she's the only one
                      Who can't escape it,
                                Her thinking intermingled
                      With the rust on a shell,
                        The crimson on a rose.

              The spoon on her wrist
                    Is feeding itself.

                         Tombstone shadows
                               Embedded in the mist,
                        Prescient,
                              Not wanting to become.

*I hope the stone forests in your amulet*
*Can heal the dead.*

Embryos or puppets or ghosts:
        What are we in the fog
    That wandered from our teacups
        To blanket Audubon Boulevard?

She peeks over the gates of Nihilism
                            To see a plow
        That wants to dig forever
                Incapable of digging by itself—
Jim Morrison had to die
        Because he didn't want to drive a tractor.

*Your waist is the perfect nook for my arm.*

             I disappear into non-history beside you:
     The world blinks,
Atomizes,
Sticking to my skin
                    Like a wet suit of microscopic eyes.

            There has never been a notion worth silence.

                Your kiss doesn't let on
            How mortal you are,
                Though I divine it
                        From the shape of your feet:
                Curved for the edges of tidepools,
                   Aquatic realms of titanic chromosomes,
                            Anemone spume,
                        Mirror-scaled snakes,
                            Watermoths,
                            A mantis of crystal,
                                Amphibious grapes,
                                    A single-celled nebula
                        Asleep in a frog's egg:
                All dreams immaterial in your breath.

            The traffic light, suspended in gauze,
                Tries so hard to speak
            But can only change its color.

        We evaporate,
            The minium borders of our bodies hushed,
            Oscillating
                Till we are only frequencies.

                        From bulb
                        To light
                        To the nerves of the eye
                        To the nerves of the wind
                        The nerves of a leaf
                        Circuit of roots

             Circuit of the palm
             The city
             The bulb
             The nerves of light:
                           Metempsychosis.

*I ran out of myself a long time ago.*

The mockingbirds are babbling about the infinite—
             It's the only thing they understand.

Thank you for leaving me to the Dawn,
             She comes now, with her diaphanous presage,
                  Powdered like a geisha,
             The tulips raise their heads
                       To smarm at her.

      *My dear, you smell better than the rain,*
      *The Dawn.*

And there you are,
      Between the rivulet of dew and a cobblestone—
And there you are:
             Gone.

## **Laura**

She's earth-green like algae:

    I found her

        Swimming in my Nalgene.

## **The Flame**

       Between her lips is a stinger:
           She shows me her body
                In the house of her lord,
                    Saying:
     *You may know the fire*
   *But you have everything to learn about the flame.*

She pins me to her mons veneris
       Then fellates me at an auto-da-fe.

# The Labyrinth of Solitude

*I see you now brother*
*As for the first time*
*You tend to your shadows*
*As I tend to mine.*

We have served so long
As men in the dust
Masters we now see
As prisoners like us:

Men chained to the flesh
And time they can't keep—
The difference between us:
We starve and they eat.

Do you remember the plaza
Where we prayed to the sun?
Stampeding fearless
Like children with guns.

The Carnival was bright,
The cannons were loud,
We died for nothing
To learn of ourselves.

We slandered our lords
To live for a day
With a violence of colors
In primal display.

We looted the temples,
Cut our hands on the gates,
We danced on the flags
Where our mothers were raped.

We laughed without joy
At all the sinners in Hell
Where every cage opens
Into a new cell.

Our hearts exploded
Like firecrackers of blood
We lived in a decadence
Of truth without love.

When the music expired,
Our nakedness played,
We regathered our masks
And revowed our shame.

*I see you now brother*
*As for the first time*
*You tend to your shadows*
*As I tend to mine.*

## **Army**

We're out on maneuvers in a rainy country, somewhere gray and verdant, with dirt trails through the hills. The sergeant explains we're here to combat a type of oracular graffiti, one that not only defaces public property, but can predict the future. There are no buildings, not even barns; we are nowhere near the city, where the real battle is being waged. Here it only rains.

Back at the mess hall a saturnal atmosphere presides. We're in no immediate danger, and our mission seems utterly pointless. We talk about our families. My sons will be two years older the next time I see them. I cry as I try to say this and the rain escapes through my tears.

**Inutil Paisagem**

Why are we fighting?
This desert's big enough for
us all to die in.

It takes desire and
sacrifice to become a
grand masturbator.

All knowing Buddha
laughs as you drink from the cup
he just now pissed in.

So tell me again:
was it your words or my ears
that were stuttering?

They smile and laugh,
start the burlesque; optimists
love a funeral.

An exposé on
door to door mattress salesmen
with nowhere to sleep.

When Earth's had her fill
she will exile all her dead
back to their fathers.

The mausoleum's
shadow, embedded in mist,
has nothing to say.

Now close my account;
I was born a beggar, it's
time I lived like one.

## A Future in Sales

Age is the peddler's enemy:
covenants made
in the shade of entwined bodies
dwindle now
that the mouth is not so comely;
now that the flesh is used, emulsified,
bleached to petrification,
and the charming guffaws
on loan from salesmanship
have yellowed
into transparent cards;
it is time to find another
as withered and incapable of being loved:
it is time to find a home.

## **Acknowledgment**

        In making love to a woman

a man forsakes every kinship,

        every oath of brotherhood.

# **Moonlight**

        I am bored of the moon—
            She will not make love to me,
    She hordes her sleep in a window
            With a guard of blue infidels
    And will not breathe it down to me—
            She is so enamored of her own perfume
    That her ivory seeds and her rain
            Forget which Earth to touch
    And which tears to cast their shawls upon.

            It is not her distance that follows me,
    Nor is it her follicles of silence
    That permeate my tamperings with the dew—
            I acquire pleasure in this irrelevance
    She prescribes to me,
            For the moon is remote, a baroness
    To those she will not receive,
            And all I want is to trespass through
    Her jealousy.

## **Letter of Sedition**

Do not forgive me for the circumstances of my personality,
    the prodigious murmurs of my delirium,
    my illusions and illuminations.
Do not forgive me for those I've distended with my hands
    nor those I've saved with my tongue,
    nor those I've unmade in my mind,
    nor those I've revived.
Do not forgive me for the forests I've laid to waste
    so our dreams could flourish,
    for worshipping the stars with the blood of a newborn,
    for torturing the oracle in her asylum,
    for walking blind into the ovens,
    for inaugurating the moth as our queen,
    for seeking refuge in her chrysalis.
Do not forgive me for being born again.
Do not forgive me, for I am a lover of things
    increate and annihilated,
    the edifice of phantoms, the ghosts of the living,
    monuments of rain, palaces of memory and air,
    photographs printed on sand, erotic mutagens.
Do not forgive me, for I am the warden of the beasts
    as I am their slave.
Do not forgive me, for I have studied your sacraments
    and I have prostrated myself
    with the weathered youths of your poverty.
Do not forgive me, for I seek not the skeleton key
    to unlock the heavens.
Do not forgive me, for we are all aligned under the constellations
    of human mythology and here we are all the same.
Do not forgive me, for my corruption breeds the pathways to
    my innocence.
Do not forgive me, for I have endured your forgiveness, stripped
    as your heir.

## **Portland**

A street like graphite, pooled with rain water, conducting an ease of context. The large cement stairs of a front stoop leading to the double doors of my friend Scott's brownstone. An old shop window filled with ancient pill bottles and vials. Sarah arrives on a motorcycle. She is tall, lean, tan: a faux punk majoring in psychology. She tells me she doesn't want anyone to know about her "thesis." I get on the back of her motorcycle. She drives me to a life-size gingerbread house in the woods. I ask how they keep it from melting in the rain. "It's made out of gingerbread," she snaps. We fuck on the lawn, completely stripped. The entire time she writes in her little black Moleskine things I cannot see; my responses, I presume.

Sarah leaves and Scott comes to pick me up. The gingerbread house is the spot where everyone new in Portland goes for their first date. He asks if the girl I'm seeing is cute. "I don't know," I respond.

We drive out in his Volvo to the Gorge, a massive cobalt canyon joining with another to form a T. The cliffs are so huge they dwarf even the mountains running the shoreline beneath: a series of pink dirt escarpments, resembling the Book Cliffs of Colorado. The sin of human psychology has been extinguished, leaving us with nothing between ourselves and the natural purity of aggregate perception. Now I have seen the reason for wonder.

Without warning Sarah appears at the top of the amphitheater. I catch her out of the corner of my eye. She wants to abduct me. Scott pretends not to notice. I excuse myself and acquiesce to her coercion. There is no resisting her.

Sarah and I are fucking on Scott's floor. I keep warning her that Scott could come home any second, but she ignores me. My body is absolutely exposed. She's pulled her pants down to her ankles, kept her shirt on, and is riding me, writing in her notebook. The situation is too loaded with anxiety to be pleasurable. I manage to climax, a development Sarah seems stimulated only intellectually by. She dismounts, dresses, and leaves, thanking me on her way out. Scott arrives. He says I look weird and asks if everything is okay. I shake my head. He smiles helplessly.

Again, the next day, Sarah shows up. She takes me down into the Gorge, where we stand in the crystalline water trying to fuck, but she can't get wet, which pleases her greatly. She records my response—my exasperation—in her Moleskine. "That's it. My paper's done," she exclaims, leaving me alone in the vast incorporeal chasm, the mountains on the shoreline growing smaller as I watch.

## **Phoenix Airport**

time is vaguely suspended
                                         yet endlessly fleeting
                  where we are
   a bomb went off today
                                   on a street in new york city
                   how shocking
an automated voice
                    drones from overhead     no smoking
     the lovely and the drab
          the average and the mad          all useless
                     all moving much too fast
   all speechless and deaf          all floating
               is it her body that moves
  or the shape of the clothes
                   that move her
      is she beautiful      or just pretending to be so
            i cant tell
she s the only one      who glows the way she does
              at this moment
does she know she stole my heart
                         as she passes out of sight
down the concourse
          her hair is dark as night
     but it s easy as the day          to forget her
               have we been old friends
or have we even met
who s to tell
                           it s always the same
play
just with different actors
                         filling in
         we mispronounce the names
of other people s gods
                 sometimes ours
the world is a mirror      smeared by the fingerprints
               of children

    when this plane takes off  
                                does the earth disappear  
or do i  
                                    we rise above the ground  
        becoming ghosts to ourselves            in the process  
                               then we come back down  
  depleted reborn anew                        in our old flesh

## **Haiku**

I broke a grass stem
then with four sturdy knots I
demanded it mend.

## **Belle**

      Step onto the carousel,
                Open your umbrella, Belle;
      This is where the evening fell,
                This is where she cast her shells.

      He sighs beneath her window sill,
                She moans, the dark, the candle quelled;
      This is where the autumn dwells:
                This is where we'll pierce their spells.

## **The Center**

Of all the places and times it was in his own hometown on the twenty-ninth of February as the rivers and sky thawed and the delirium tremens of the night before finally subsided that he found the Center.

She poured coffee into his cup with her left hand while balancing plates on the flat palm of her right, answering the questions of the other waitresses, who were much older than she, with the poise and dignity of a mother who knows and comforts. She was sixteen, the same age his grandmother had been when she'd married his grandfather. Her eyes were chestnut, her hair flaxen, her lips uncanny in their common smiles. When he looked at her he saw settler women wresting food for their families from the mountain winter, then in their rocking chairs with hand-stitched quilts on their laps, never having relented to the petty usury of the world. She had the ingenuity that only a being capable of carrying another life inside them can possess; the tenderness that belongs to those who wish only to feed others.

*That was America,* he said.

This wasn't the first time he'd seen the girl. He'd been to this diner before. He knew the men who would come in and sit at the counter just to see her; to imagine how devoted they would be to her, raising in their minds a muffled Eden where she would understand the good in them and they could treat her with all the kindness in their hearts, all the kindness no one else would allow.

He finished his coffee, got up, and turned towards the door, thinking that her eyes were on him as he walked out. The daylight greeted him pure and transparent. He thought that it was the first day of spring, then he thought that he would come back to the diner tomorrow if the day was as beautiful; but even then, if all was as untarnished and perfectly laid as it was now, it would still only be the second day of spring.

### **Invocation**

     O lotus or irradiant names!
  Dalliance of birth dreams through immortal spectrums!
    Let me remain a beggar always
      In the unfolding mercy of your petals—
    In the neon sweat of your tendrils
      Let me draw my last breath!

# **Requiescat**

Exiled figments:

The camera never stops:

To Lyvinia,
        Half nascent,
    Drawing light from the earth
    And water from the sky for her bath;
Iris,
    Whose eyes are dreamt twins;
Lucy,
    Turning the pages in an atlas of imaginary shadows;
Kate,
    With her shoulders naked,
    Misquoting a song from the radio;
C,
    With words hidden in other words,
    Her moods dictating the tincture of her fingernails;
Maria,
    Clamoring drunk up the stairs,
    Always searching her purse for the telephone—
    A million unseen partners;
E,
    Vermiculated, sunbathing
    In the stone compositions of winter
    To the lust of her brother;
Janice,
    The floating confines of the future;
Victoria,
    Orbiting birds grow thirsty,
    Attaining then re-attaining your virtue;
And to M,
    And the velvet swimming
    Of the cosmos between her thighs.

## **Transcription of a Lotus Vine in Memphis**

The fire dreams,
        The spring shrinks into itself,
A single flower explodes,
        A thousand invisible birds die in its song.
The river floods from her pores
        And she drowns in herself.
She exhales a dove.
        A palace of thimbles quakes
And never ceases to collapse.
        I incinerate her lotus with my lips;
She bleeds inside the sun;
        She cums, annihilated in its grain;
Eternity poses for our lovemaking:
        The world is begging for our sex.
The game of masks and nudity,
        Aspects and fragmentations,
Mirrors; despotism and pity;
        Fountains where we bathed cutting their throats for us,
Their tears crystal fusing with the Word,
        The war hymn in her vulva
Quaking like an open palm
        Transfiguring blood into amethyst;
All the creases, the garnet leaking from the tip of her—
        Begging to watch me
Watch.
        All the bodies we inhabit
Decaying, the pain
        An emblem of beauty
Denied at the apex,
        The catastrophe of perfectly merged flesh
Discarnate, fomenting
        The spines in a lush network
The parallel eruption that feeds them
        Corrupts from the crest.

## **Carry Me Down**

       Swift neon signs flash out your horoscope—
         The plateau's verge—
               The depth of blue phosphoresce
            In the cat eyes
        Along the border—
             Hotels ride the wind—
         A sky entranced in absentia—
         A plea—

Carry me down
Past the burning crosses
              And turning fields of wheat—
     Where mother buried the soldiers' bones
         And hymnal;
  Hell rises from the corn
      In the slaves' field;
           I know I am seeing a nocturnal flower
              Open for the last time—
         I know the worms
          Indulge—

    Dusk has a heart
        In every voice grown silent
          And my voice has grown
           With the dusk—

Carry me down,
                  Besmirched,
                 Beleaguered,
                   Beguiled—

Carry me down,
        To the Beggar every grain of sand is a sun,
          Grant me the courage to be so poor—
    If tears come

Carry me down—
The mountains fissured below the horizon—
    The oilpool displays of the harvest—
        The tar looked on by a thousand satellites—
            The hummingbird turning into a salamander
                In the hand of the exile—
            The eagle with its nest in the marsh—
              The locust drowning in nectar,
                  Topaz, delphinium—

Carry me down,
        The honey consumed by the hallowed moth—
            The panther in the reeds—
              The silver tablets
                  Of the dragonfly's wings—

Carry me down,
        After the final tremors have departed—
            Where the darkness of who we are radiates
            Though the light unfolds its arms to reach us—

Carry me down—

Carry me down,
        Give form to the mystery;
            The vultures of Christ
                Bedecked in the memory of our blood
                    Stand against our witness—
            The palms of his hands:
                What clay or water or smoke will recognize
The cordiform tracery of their lines?

Carry me down,
    Where no rest awaits us.
    The deer awaits no rest,
    The hunter sleeps,
    The bow in his tongue tinder,
    Inexhaustible.

## A Brief Prayer

May your gods watch over you tonight
    Whatever their names may be.

## **The Epiphany**

Her warm blossom and peppermint
liturgy astound the tanning wheat
and lacquered apples of her supple
physiognomy. She thought her brain
a mere functional commodity now a
miracle of biblical purport has
discovered to the audience she can move
her mouth to make statements with
a certain selectivity akin to genius. Her
most serene cogitations suddenly
leave her disparaged as she sees the ruin
of her body the unmitigated history of
her mind will bring.

## The Ballad of Anna Nicole Smith

I was subsisting off Slim Fast,
      Yogurt, butter, and methadone,
When I passed
      From this calamitous world
            To the next.
      A certain demographic
          Wed in pity and fascination
      A fantasy
          To see how naked
             Death got
  On my body
             Perfected.

No oil tycoon,
        No cattle baron,
           Only the mortician
        Can take pictures of me now.

Special report
    For the hordes
  Of the bored and the monogamous:
Kleenex on sale
      Next to the candles.

What about the microscopes?

What about the purity
We were promised at birth?

## **Nurse's Song**

As the migrants of youth we stole wedding songs
          And covenants of topaz:
     Our vows we strung through the wake of the dawn
     In the trill, without thought, unabashed.

Moments of beauty must soon be repaid
          To laws that none can forestall:
     When the marriage sublime consumes the day
     The night will make widows of us all.

## **Haiku**

        The heat of Nature

                ushers from our bones' marrow

the first sighs of Spring.

## **Nostopathy**

abandoned
you reenter
the bedroom
where in youth
mother
harnessed your
winces fed
you to her
medicine
out of
love there
is no
prophecy every
shadow a
stranger
waiting to
break open
a candle
waiting to
distill the
frontier
of soot
the men
worshipped
pederasts
the women
lost
deformed
by an inebriate
virtue

## **To a Master**

    We were listening
        As your shattered days progressed
    Like servants with their heads bowed
        Through the hallways of space.
We were listening
        In our amnesia
    Eager for proof of your silence
        And your surrender.
We were listening
        With our hands and our eyes
    And our tongues tied with lace.
We were listening
        To the footfalls of your pilgrimage
    Under a sun of mortal and passing flesh.
We were listening
        And moaning,
    Stricken in the bed of our lover
        And in the beds of our lovers.
We were listening
        To the temporal cadence of your violins,
    Their timbre in the first apparition.
We were listening
        In our brothels and our school halls,
    In our kitchens and our courthouses.
We were listening
        For a material orgasm
    To shiver the goddess,
        For her sublime nadir.

We were listening and we heard you.

        We were listening and now we are singing,
The report of your trumpets and our bodies
        Flicker in and out of the magnet's echo.
We sing the demons of gods
        Drawn through the celerity of man;

We sing the whispers of doves
> Who carry torrents in their mouths;
We sing that someday our thirst may be quenched;
We sing there is only one illusion
> And that is divinity;
We sing every human heart beating as one;
We sing the night moving the sedge
> Through the thieves;
We sing the first words praying for the last;
We sing the thunder of stars battering the ground
> After watching them slip down the sky
> Soundless as corsets;
We sing the rumble of comets
> In Kṛṣṇa's belly:

We sing the clamor of skeletons
> As they drape themselves in velvet
> To prepare for the ball.

## A Religious Trifle

      Heaven is not a temple
      The seeker shall attain:
      Heaven is a junkyard
      We build on our miseries
      So others may find bliss.

## For Our Lady, a Nocturne

I

      She collects men around her
And she tames them with music,
She addresses them in tongues,
Our transcendent procuress;
Dignitaries waltz in her rays and her shadows,
The Olympians spy from the shrouds of their corners,
And her ventriloquists play their parts,
No matter the needles she stabs in their dolls,
No matter the hours they must shiver alone.
      Are they her friends or grandiloquent strategists
Pronouncing fate as they see it spelled out before them,
Asking themselves if this is their doom or their destiny
To trace these intellectual labyrinths
That leave the roots of our consciousness
Twisted as the sand at the bottom of her riverbed
Yet smooth as the opal
In the basin of her turtle shell?

      O how she plucks the bones like a mandolin player,
Her kittens fall right in line so prayerful to heed her,
Dressing their trumpets in her flags and her standards—
      Angles form and are married to the moment
      As the word is wed to the weight of the image—
Here my literature lays like a kiss at her doorstep
As I am dragged by the horns through the haze of her spring,
To be sacrificed atop this plateau of her invisible desert;
Through his personal wasteland
Here Lawrence strings his acolytes to their deaths,
His destitute triumphal presage:
I swear by whatever laws she accords from this day forward
I will bow to and speak only of her luminescence,
      No matter the cost,
For as long the sea folds its shoals beneath her whaling ships
      And miracles interrupt matter,

Laughing with all the pastel starfish
Fossilized on her coral reef.
    Let me draw in the rose's blood
    A Madonna to afflict us all.
  While we're locked in the stages of our quiescence:
      The key to all existence
      Though plainly set before us
      Vanishes when it senses
      The possession of our touch.

      Have you met her, my son?
  She dissipates in rarefied atmospheres:
    The mind magicians:
History prefigures itself in her gales
As the lances of her warriors plunge
Through the top of her circus tent.
Let me dangle from the hem of her merciless illusion
For I see all that dies had once to be born there;
Let her swallow me whole in codified verses
As we translate our bodies from this form to the next.

My pen runs dry with ways to name the Sphinx,
    The tigress turns to woman in the imperial ruins:
    Praise be to the delicate majesty of her eyelids,
    Her eyelashes that bend like bejeweled cricket legs,
    How she gathers ethereal objects to taunt and to tease us;
    Time grows from the eucalyptus in her bedroom;
    Festival catalogues indecipherable as promised;
In her cipher we're all vagabonds
Coercing the puppets of our knowing
Like milk-colored moths
Branded with fire
Escaping the first lights
Of dawn.
    Her lovers cling to the curve of her wrist
    Like coins drawn towards the arch of a magnet;
    Like rosewood beads she ties them around her
    Stroking them with the softest parts of her palms;

Her electric music box gives birth to distorted symphonies,
        Plainchants and choral odes
As she sifts through the ash filled goblets of former incantations
For our sacrament:
    A ghostly brassiere hangs in the wardrobe of her memoirs;
Behind the blue whistles and incandescent globes of Eternity
        The story of the world is displayed
            Like a map stitched from bearskin rugs;
    Before our queen of transmutations
    The earliest myths etched on the lizard's scales
    Shuffle down the corridor
    Clanking their armor
    And banging their swords on their shields;
        Dragons amass in the ice-chilled opium vapors
           Of her particolored glass.

She never wears much to distinguish her body
From the water that hangs so dense in the Tennessee air;
Like quicksilver she slips from the loveseat
And in a huff and a puff of nitrous she dissolves,
Leaving a green jaguar in her stead,
The russet moss blooming in her stairwell
That can only be the color of her hair.
Accordions, harmoniums, instruments without name
Seek each other in the gothic light of her aquarium garden.
All paths of flight lead only to the mist
Where it is your duty to elude her.

                II

    You may not think it is so,
    But I cry for every heart I break
    And every road I take grows longer.
        That is why it grieves me so
        That Madame Keciorius
        Has not yet learned
        To cloak herself within her camera:
In this dim memory she begs for the versified code

To combine her body with mine
           And all I can do is refuse her:
None of my gifts can soothe her now
With her thoughts transparent,
      Rending their faces, their breasts,
Like wasps they tear and stab at me as I am forced to enact them.
      Line by line, bit by bit,
Until both the actor and the audience lose their sight.

      *You can't go home again,*
I have always been told this
          But why should I burn at the stake
          For assuming the role of the gentleman?
Why was it my lot to be crucified on the altar of her silence
              As she pleads to an eidolism?
      She pursues me,
She boils my heart in the tar her sadness quickens.
          I am not the teacher to absolve or demean her
          Or lift the burden she churns beneath her skirt.
Now she is Lopita, stroking her nimble felines
Atop a mountain of digested machines.
          But oh, how she doesn't see it.

        Yet to you,
With your hair the color of the first flames,
     She is ripe and the talons have yet to sink in.
         Would we both like to believe
K. exists solely for the mind of some jade-draped prince
     Who will ravish her
         Atop a white-feathered parapet?
In her kingdom there is no architecture
    And the omens of her harps ring as empty as they do vast;
It sounds like suicide every time she closes
            The door to her chamber where she lurks
Like the Empress of Maids.
She will never be invited to unravel my notebooks
Nor piece together the vagaries of weather that control my past,
Nor do I wish upon her a pure glimpse of the savageries

And solitudes that control our everyday lives,
        But, oh, how I cannot ignore that she sees them—
She's too well acquainted with the manner in which
Our meager daily productions, when mixed
With the tragical element of love, erupt,
Laying to fiction our average routines,
The mute dynasty of common disguises,
Leaving all touched in the wake
            Maimed, despoiled, and unredeemed.
Her gaze falls on me like an X-ray that thinks in my bones
        And there is no way to avoid it;
This is what consumes me, for I desire only her solace
      But will never be as close as she would have me;
I am not the one to cherish the length of her legs
      Nor the texture of her skin,
          Though I pray she finds him
And is never confined to the museum of his life's work.

### III

My pen, the demons, austere and human,
      The cowards,
The angels disintegrating there, will, henceforth
Manifest only in your service:
      A composition of celestial mortality.
I pay homage to the fountain of your hands,
For I have drank of all things there,
Both physical and increate;
My throat has been scalded;
The stars have been healed by astrology.
Let your other jesters
Make the snakes of the cosmos purr.

How could I know these theatre-red walls
      Would usher me to such sublime condemnation
In the limbs of your olive tree?
      How could I decipher the trajectory of the mosaic,
The divine travesties under your grand colonnades

    As you lifted the blinds
        You secret the moon behind?

I was forged from the dust to bear the crucible of the poor,
To weave this iridescent catacomb for you to wander;
I search for the sacred representations of reality,
If reality is sacred:
        *I see that your body is free,*
        *It is your veils that are promiscuous.*

I demand what the fantasy demands of me.

## **OM**

All things are sacred
As all things are lost.

### William Faulkner — American Author: 1897 — 1962

Here and now we begin our journey into the heart of America.

(This record is not intended to illuminate the future, nor could it be purported to accurately depict the present. Like all humans, the author is bound exclusively to the distortions of the past; the prejudices, the stupidity, the knowledge and occasional wisdom they present him. Time is the only chimera capable of drawing on the sun the landscapes and figures meagerly stitched into this manuscript's perpetual dusk.)

In the mandala
Every premonition is an echo.

# Out of the Ether

*Fuck life.*

~Samuel Beckett

**A Day in the Dust**

Praise to the rabble,
The wretched and the wanton;
Praise to the scorpion's sting;
The bees who keep their hives
Tidy and paralyzed
Like housewives with orders to clean;
Praise to gamblers,
The dice, the cards,
Their eyes sucking the light
From the cocktail waitress' smile;
Praise to fire in the year of revolution;
Praise to veils and lanterns,
Claws dim against the glass,
Faces hidden and those barely exposed;
Praise to salt in the king's cup,
His starved fiefdom;
Praise to frogs and pollywogs and cracked teeth and yellow
Sclera;
Praise to the kindergarten teacher's liver bleeding
As her students look on,
The crimson threads snagging on the wind;
Praise to the jaguar's skin taut over his muscles
As he grabs the doe by her neck;
Praise to the lightning of elements enraged;
Praise to the ghost swallowing the mine;
And praise to these dolls of wax
Who live but do not breathe and do not die.

# **A Pensive Moon Is Glued to the Shatterproof Sky**

you play the mother's sparkling
eyes in the hallway you play
the nervous fly in the year
of the spider I'll play
the benumbed ambulance
driver bedridden through the second
coming of Caesar
Antichrist the texture of Infinity
collected in a crimson
spiral now you play
your body as a cloak and a
dagger in the hour of black
hyacinths transposed the
temple spire's castrated
trunks you spray your
holocaust and every
drop hangs a polished
pendulum in the air
a fever aquiver a
single mirror pushing
backward now you play
the ashes the pale pink
scar the porcelain doll
strangling her evening
like she promised like
a tablet in water a
star jaundiced as the day you
were born weaving in out
of all others a
radioactive birth
without birth
without

## **An Opal Dream**

An impenetrable calligraphy of masks and curtains;
A floating cathedral of incandescent fetuses;
The omnific Cardinal unleashes his brood
Over all the Earth:

> *Glory to the highest reality!*
> *Glory to the sweat of the clouds!*
> *May they pour forth into our hands*
> *The molecular vision*
> *Of Discontinuity and Connectedness!*

All things in the ultraviolet;
The prism holds sway as it opens its eyes;
The laughter in strings
Born over and over
Through contrasting patterns
The composition resumes.

## How to Tone Your Belly & Thicken Your Glutes

Eternal rules
For Gods and Fools:
Be kind to those
Cast from the fold.

Do not forget
We're made of dust:
Some resplendent,
Some ravenous;

Some born vultures;
Some born as doves;
Compliant or
Contumacious;

Some born to lead
The flesh to greed
Then burn the bones
Like so much coal;

They use the truth
To snare with words
Sovereign lovers,
Helpless warlords.

Desert gardens
Demand the praise
Of simpletons
From high estates;

But those born in
The sunbaked lodge
Know the verdant
To be mirage.

Though palpable,
Amiable,
Here a garden
Wreaks malfeasance.

It seems the truth
Of facts and proofs
Yet it is not
In one's own heart:

It is a lie
Imposed from high
On those they see
As meek and mean.

And those below,
Turned from the fold,
Will see the gift
As slanderous;

A hateful joke;
A cruel insult;
A garish bunt
Or low affront.

Be kind to those
Turned from the fold
But don't attempt
To redeem them;

By force or wit
Enlightenment
May not concern
The ones you've spurned.

Be kind to those
Turned from the fold

But don't impose
Your lavish yoke.

Be kind to them
Who can't submit
But let them be
What they're to be.

## **The Megalomaniac's Satire**

W.S. Burroughs said this:

*Legends of the West enfold this planet.*

       The Sundance Kid is
a prepackaged reflection—
   A boiling spring in the seas of the
sun.

  Who hasn't longed for the soiled wedding
veil
    & the nickel-plaited six gun?

     The West is just a facsimile of
itself—
A hallucination compiled from the remnants of a
stage set.

   (The jaundiced howl of a coyote
    sifted through an epoch of sage brush).

      The petticoated Miss
tosses from the train
     her embroidered
handkerchief as you,
    trotting beside, offer her
the roseless thorn.

   A fire wakes in the sand

beside the carriage.

## Mrs. Brambleberry's Psychotic Niece

If you fear the tortures you'll receive
For exposing the officials of humanity
What do you think the gods will do
If your wandering gaze happens to
Penetrate their private conference;
If the light that spawns all light fills up their robes
Like the sun illuminates the dress of a girl
Who stands by the window in summer
Outlined in a nakedness and perfection
You were never meant to see and all that remains
Is an eternity for you to be punished?

## **Happiness Is King**

The Seasons keep council in the eyes of the babe
                As you marry your hand to mine;
May there be peace in both lantern and hearth
                As he sleeps by the fire tonight.

## **Clearview Townhouses for Sale**

        ] Welcome to our island community [

] Shirtless gladiators with chainsaws carve dolphins out
   of
                                              rosewater icicles [

      ]     Last year's ginger Palm Tree Princess sips a
daiquiri
                              exhibiting her pink
                              age-speckled skin    [

      ] Neptune poses with his ivory trident immaculate [

                    ]    Miss Leper USA passes out balloons
                                  till she strains a
hamstring   [

     ] Gymnasts with videogames inside them
              bronzing their carpal tunnel [

]    Oblivion and the
                        indigenous world    [

## Easy Millions

        !!!!!!!!!   I WANNA SEE FORMAL WEAR
& BANQUET DINNERS FOR THE POOR MAN   !!!!!!!!!

Why?

Because I don't have a single pissed up cent in my pocket
              And I don't have a clue as to how I'm supposed
to budget $700 a month to live on when it costs $600 for a shitty one bedroom apt.

        Is this the REGULAR BASIS?

    Do me a favor:
                Use my skeleton as a coupon
            To purchase a Fabergé toilet.
                I'm interested in heredity.

Could you wring out my brain with a primary election?

      I've been told I was once enlightened out of necessity
              But now I've tuned into this shoddy fourwaystop
satellite channel reality and I want the whole discography

Being broke just ain't thrilling the ladies anymore
How can I open 'em up and shut 'em like a closet door?
I have nothing new to remark on        whatever war
I'm a good fakir,
Damn dumb down to the core,
I don't eat cologne,        I live in a different time zone
I don't have pity enough to laugh at my own jokes
My landlady is counting the days till I get croaked
I am master of only the infantile obtuse rhyme
And I have somehow been convinced
That despite the cost to myself and those I love
No matter the sacrifice
I can't stop
Farting.

## **Treat Me to Dinner, Louise**

3 a.m. stilettos

this electric diner

drips through the window

a motel sign in nowhere

turns frost all it touches

and mist all it cannot

the street a river

departing

walking through a honeymoon

she had to rent

she came here a child

and now leaves

with her last bounced check

## **Glowering**

Think of all the dusk would say
If she found you courting the dark this way,
In your raiment of light, your language of gold,
Begging the shadow's ilk to unfold—
Surely she would not be pleased.

And what would be her response
To the stroke of your palm's diurnal fronds
Across the faces of her slaves in their yokes?
She'd crush you with soot as with stone:
She is well-known for her greed.

## **Vacancy**

                Tangerine atoms seep through the
morning;
                Hands of mercury etch bodiless
heavens;
                Unguided languages in silhouette
procession;
                City windows: a rain beguiled
illusion;
                Bronze strings, electric, leak through the
floorboards;
                A scarab on the ring of her lover
alights;
                A lunar eclipse dissolves in the
doorway;
                The wind
coughs;
                A tumbleweed unravels the
desert.

## The Man Wearing My Face

I ask now to be released from your Heavenly Father,
He that sees and touches all yet sees and touches nothing:
No more of his sanguine virtue and epicene pleasure;
No more through the circuits of forced poverty and tithe.

'Neath his celestial haunts and his bone dry palaces
I've wandered through his neophytes and his catechumen,
Begging a drop of spit to fill up the chalices
I was born to hold, though too heavy for human hands.

I ask now to be released from my mind, body, and soul:
I would rather be a desert pinion or a juniper;
To think none of it yet hold communion with the whole;
Burdened not with words to say the entire Universe.

**Various Corporate Hideouts & Headquarters**

I fought on both sides of the revolution.

## **To Be Is to Belong**

Though I've had
A double mastectomy
I'm free
I'm free
From my body
It can no longer harm me
All is vanity
All is vanity
Oh to be anything
Oh to be anything
Is to belong

### They're Peaking

In the end, our captain chose to come down the mountain alone, behind the rest of us; not because he couldn't keep up, nor was he incapable of leading: he simply did not want us to see the way his boots slipped on the smooth wet stones.

### You, Me & All Those Lucky Ladies

Your heart is a transparent epigraphy.
I want to construct an anagram
Between your voice and silhouette.
I want to superfetate the currents of your tongue.
I want to genealogically catalogue the palettes of your flesh.

## **Intrigue Is King**

Outburst of silence in the vehicle of words:

Reason's area dragged through continual purpose.

                      Throbbing ideal of gravity:
Indifference.

               *We here at The Oppressed*
*Weightlessness have other plans for you:*
               *1st we start with the diet:*
               *Metabolize nylon crisis papers in*
*the swoon voice of sometimes salient,*
                    *the bored compendiums eking out*
*their own sorrowful*           *postsubstantiations—*
      *!!!!!!DON""T PREACH TO US*
*about the wordless macrominimalism*
               *or you'll find yourself sentenced to 25*
     *accelerations*
               *on the deincapsapitulator!!!*
                    *We prefer words*
*w/out bodies to express themselves*
     *through transmissions of sleep and don't get*
*us started*
               *on the voice wearied*
*syllogram!!!!!*

## **Milkshake Avenue**

            I remember waking up next to you
            On Milkshake Avenue,
            Coughing hollyhocks and daffodils yawning
            When morning stretched herself pale
            Across our bodies in the bed.
            In a dream I look down on us
            Then turn around to gaze up at the sky
            Noticing it's the color of your eyes.
How strange to say
I remember waking up next to you
When neither of us ever awoke
From our little kingdom
On Milkshake Avenue.

## Three Maudlin Marys & Their Sick Puppy

*How far must we venture
  Before courage pays our debts?*

*How well are we acquainted
With the ones who took our bets?*

*The world is a casino
We're all buying off the feds*

*(though some of us are in bed
    with the president
of the Las Vegas, Nevada
Gaming Commission).*

## The Mendicant Daughter

        She's a book I've put on the shelf
        Promising myself one day to read
        But all those magazines...
        They're strippers.

She dresses like a girl without a name:
        Plain Jane.
It's a shame to lose at your own game,
        Plain Jane.
You were born to play how you play,
        Plain Jane.
You need to find someone to lose with you your way,
        Plain Jane.

## **Coughing Tulips Saved My Life**

       Words betray because they are human:
           Music cannot
  For it is Godly.

## **Cleanliness Is Key**

The world is congested with histories.
Too many objects have adopted personae
And now demand to enter the citizenry.
Automobiles are mistaken for clergymen.
Stilettos and combat boots are holding
A congressional hearing on censorship.
The calendars roll their eyes.
A legion of devoted cookbooks
Forget to drop their kids off at school.
Manic depressive hairnets
Mix cocktails.
Carpets produce their own sitcoms.
The empire of manufactured goods
Will soon replace The Kingdom of Man.
We must accept the facts.
We are being run off this planet
By silverware and crockery,
Microwave ovens that can recite the *Wall Street Journal*.
If we wish to maintain control we must devolve—
To the monkey then the houseplant
Then the primordial snot—
Only there shall we defeat ourselves and our creations
To finally harvest an image of G-d
Within.

## My Pants Are Following Me

Welcome to a who's who of
    nobodies        and unoriginals
and the movie    started    without you.

## **Eegad, I've Been Nabbed**

Do not grow accustomed to miracles.

## A Thousand Degrees Below Zero

Oh brilliant sun that is the word *Forever*!
      The promise of everlasting virtue
      Reflected in your mirror
      Dwindles now like a star
      Accosted by the vices of night!

Oh brilliant sun
          Now reprised in the semblance of *Never*!
      I pursue the whims of your chastity
      Like so many slivers of light,
      Unsatisfied to dwell within the impermanence
      Of that baleful word *Forever*!
      I seek the purity of the reflection
      That touches not the mirror—

## A Thousand Degrees at Zero

I'm glad you didn't die
Before I could remember
Though it would have been easier
Though it would have been easier
For both of us.

Your red haired daughter says
She knows you're resting with Jesus
(You died before she could remember)
But wouldn't it be simpler
If she could see you?

## **A Thousand Degrees Until Zero**

If gods there be behind those clouds,
Unwilling to be touched, unfound,
Should faith in their mercy be the choice?
To pleas fearing their glory should we be bound?

If gods behind those clouds there be
Their eyes fall not on you or me,
They provoke us not to act nor rest
Nor tame us with nuances of destiny.

If there be gods behind those clouds,
Forgotten thus within their shrouds,
Knowing only light that has no voice,
With silent stones they speak to both meek and proud.

If behind those clouds gods there be,
Gold arrayed, their only deed
To balance love equal with distress
It would seem just as well if no gods there be.

## **Look 'em in the Eye Before You Shoot**

when i was born words broke and every warden got religion
                          the book:
              scripture of the fragile eternity

1984 prisoners ran amuck through the pages
jeering and braying and chipping their teeth on
the bars

                      ain t no facts to prove it
                    just raw animal intuition
            beasts know the year i was spawned
strands of naked essence like celestial stamens
              beribboned the sewers as flowers bloomed there
wilting coral sunburned marigolds turned to dust
          and pink dandelions opened up to drink the sewage

              i wasn t planted i was forged
      from a goat s horn and a whale s bone   :
i wasn t frozen      sleeping      pacified
though i was silent
       it was tranquility rubbed my belly and
kissed my toes
            as the pestilent legions rioted
      in the pissstench schoolhouses

there was bile in the topiary halls
for the moment i was conceived
i was made tired to disown
                our human consumptive energy

there was embalming fluid in the bowels of
architecture the first time i breathed

## The CIA in Honolulu

*Clarice, look, I_m going on vacation to Acapulco
and I need you to pick up some things for me:*

*Four Mexicans: one to pour my margaritas
into the shaker, another to shake, a third to
pour the margarita into the glass, and the last
to salt and lemon the ridge, maybe even a
fifth to hand it to me since the fourth is already
pulling double duty.*

*One Uncle Tom nigger to play harmonica
for me*
        *while I shit*
*and read bedtime stories.*

*Seven corn-bred southern frat boys to tell
me how big their dicks are and how many
bitches they_ve fucked in the ass*
                *with their daddy's*
 *rig.*

*Finally, twelve towelheads to tell me I look*
      *good in this tie.*

*Oh yeah, I almost forgot, I need a hundred
thousand slant-eyed Nagasaki shadows to*
      *syphon my cum through a Cub Scout textbook.*

*If you could have all of this ready by tomorrow
morning that'd be great.*

*Oh, and uh, tell Dave I send him my most
heartfelt condolences for his fiftieth.*

## **Steadfast Willy & the Gang**

       To my orphan family:
Mothers, sisters, fathers, brothers,
Shylock priestesses and bishops
In rags and soot-stained shawls;
Nieces and nephews of the rails
Huddled around a sugar skull,
A Judas valentine,
On this day in February
Wilting like
The zinc on the hand of the widow,
      The wedding locket.
      I've gathered you here
Not to plan for future elopements,
Nor to arrange penance for the past,
But to offer you thanks
For the strange forms of love you've given me
          And to declare:
      I need your peculiar displays of affection
          No longer.

## Chocolate Merchant Dies Young

Every morning I wake to the buzzing of a fly
caught between my window and the blinds,
frenzied, battering itself against its own reflection.
I can never swat it and lately
              I don't even try.

The dog's tail slaps my door,
        his paws patter on the linoleum
        as I attempt to ignore
        the prying fingers of the sun.
I hack up, my tongue
        feels like a clot of gum
        chewed in someone else's mouth,
        then back into sleep I am sunk.

        I live on a dead end street
        far from Milkshake Avenue
        where, as a door-to-door chocolate merchant,
        I paid my dues.

There's nothing serious about the candy business,
        but God how I wish I would have kissed
        at least one of those Easter-eyed girls
        who met me on her porch
        with her cheeks round and blushing
        fine as peaches in their fervor of Sunday down.

        The candy business isn't that interesting.

All I have these days is too much time to ask myself
why I'll always prefer the fruit I'll never taste
to easily unwrapped chocolate.

## Charlie's Doppelgänger's Doppelgänger

        DeLi.verance means:
                              CaT ,ATONic nigh.tshift
heaD.a.ches
                Tap-ered continually w/
OXY.c.h.a.g.r.i.n;
                                  white espad;ille
hol;days
                  & bleach-ed tunics muffled inthe
Amoxicillin
l_a_m-plight;
                F----------r----ocks and ca___rd;g=ns
                    of mobile (
) home beige and
                  saccharine wallp
                aper sermonious in modeled
plaster lawn
                            a.c.T.i.V.ity.
                        n0tI0nle$s
br;degroom [con { (substantiation]) :
    the garden hose and the gardener :

## **Not One Iota of Remorse**

I have nothing to say and I intend to prove it.

## The Suitable Advance

A citrine waltz;
An amethyst gardenia;
Fragrance of agate;
Turquoise birthwater.

The sculptor's marble;
The diamonds of a torture;
Lime from the catacombs;
Granite from the prison.

## Your Record Shows

The silhouette of a girl named Iris;
Three emerald feathers from a peacock's eyelids;
A tulip from the lapel of a gameshow host;
A broken cigarette on the stem of a rose.

Two shoddy quatrains and a Venus of snow;
Asp-headed bangles for the burlesque girl;
Orozco's Christ in a chalice of sand;
A mirror the shape of a newborn's hand.

## **Nettle Calsworthy, Loyal Practitioner**

Are you mocking me in front of my mail order bride?
Are you judging me because she's twice my height?

>Your scrutinizing gaze
>Stabs the softest points of my skin;
>You know the topography well,
>Go on, stick your thumbtacks in.

Do you point at me and say, *There's his mail order bride?*
Do you feel like a man when you say I'd lose to her in a fight?

>I pick up on your insinuations,
>I wake up and I care what you think,
>But believe me when I tell you, mister,
>—and this is a delicate point of pride—
>She may not be much to look at
>>But she's *my* mail order bride.

## **Impossibly Cool & Distant**

                                                                           Long night,
Posing as a dishwasher in a disheveled
subterranean
                      Frozen dinner factory.

I step outside for a smoke break and it's raining.

My brain swims with the evaporation of
tail lights,
The blue murmur of tires over tar-veined asphalt,
                            The perspiring ghosts of stars,
            Then I'm searching for my body in a panic.

The thought comes to me that any form will do
        So I slip into an orchid and coalesce with
the water
                    I'm leaching from the ground.

            The opiate musk of ivory and the immutable
                  Bitter moldering of iron overwhelm me
Through the autumn's gossamer solvent
        As everything becomes luminous and near
Yet impossibly cool and distant
                In the inkblack neon
                              of Time's mouth.

## **Don't Placate the Dolphins**

This planet is a spinning prison the blankspace subterranean martians indemnified in their acrostic philology implement through digital coercion policies soporific and accelerant to cross stitch the boardrooms of the profiteering indigent anatomies who abbreviate our souls with their slogans and their hypercritical apostrophe eyes.

## **Welcome to My Hallucination**

       I watch the blackhearted vanguard comedians
Entering the hierophant;
       I watch the candymadman lick the nimble
Excrement next door;
          Above me the Lords of Peace
                Cavort with the Gods of War—
I've got fifteen dollars, baby,
*Take me to the liquor store!*
            Your thongs wet on Venus,
        I'm as hard as a thundercloud on Mars;
We are the blood fuming through the veins
of the lonely shepherd's heart—
We're mutts braying in our cages—
We're piranhas in a bowl— We're
*LUNATICGEARCLANGMAROONEDAMPHETAMINESAXA
PHONES!!!!!!!*
                         Shut the door, honey,
                             Look the other way,
              I've got a bone-yellow violin
              Dr. Osiris taught me how to play!
                It's getting tight in here,
                Let's move out to the lake,
We'll set those geriatric cabins
                    & gentile docks ablaze!
                      Pay your taxes early,
              Make friends with the warden—
She's always been and always will be
              My favorite illegitimate:
                  I'd let her cut my foreskin;
                  I'd let her shovel my ashes
            Out of Auschwitz
With a paper mask sagging
            Down to her kneecaps—
Blue eyebrows, onyx specimens and pearl spoons:
    Cast the winning veto!

Smack your lips and pound your tail
*En flagrant* in your swine colored coat!
There's a boar's head on the love seat,
There's a camel in the tub,
There's a moldy lotus petal
Drying in the sun—
        Put a plastic bag over your head—
        Sink your feet deep in the bog—
        Chaw a plug of dogfood soufflé—
                Get born again in a barn—

## **Mob Boss Devours 3-Ton Meatball, Makes Peace with Local Cops**

                sterilized zombies on mind patrol
                concentration camps
                constantinople

our brooms are tired of sweeping

                saprophyte prophets design control
                biometric stamps
                constant in opal

our truth's expired from weeping

## **Tender as a Thorn**

      I long to gaze up God's green skirt,
To view the impeccable squash of her nether regions
& the murmuring tomatoes at the hinge of her thighs,
      To see what has never been hidden,
To see what I will never be forgiven for seeing.

## **Shrimp Boats Bring Home the Bacon**

                    Praise to these disaffecters!
Pseudo-Illuminists drafting
     the second hand smoke of vision!
They !!!!!!!!!*REEEAALLYYY*!!!!!!!!! feel this way—
                      Let them tell you
        at the public daycare center of poetry
where mediocre fights vacuous for the trophy lunch
                            & nothing is felt
                            & nothing stirs
        under the drapery of ascetic light
     where the lunatic jungles have been clearcut
& the toll to cross into ourselves has been
outsourced
                    & car wheels drone
        across the endless stripmined thread
     of a highway that will never be forged.

## **No, I Don't Want to Meet Your Boyfriend**

   Your boys come to you from their arcades
     On the foals of Hyperion,
    Crying, *Eleutheria*!
       Shirtless with sunburned shoulders.

You say they are shameless,
How they hold the reigns of Apollo in their hands—

   Your boys coerce you till their throats sting,
     But you judge them on pedigree:
    A smooth flesh panoply
      Kronos calls his champion.

You say they are meek,
Each can only entertain you for a moment—

   Your boys, in chains, you bend like wet clay;
     Your miracles at apogee
     Hold the wanton ancestry
      Eros enslaves to his ends.

You say they are helpless,
As now you find yourself kneeling to their commands—

   Your boys call to you as their moon wanes—
     Fossils bordered in minium—
     The rain tastes of Ilion—
      Night leaves naked all she nurtures.

You say they are weak
But your nymph's thirst knows what their whispers portend—

## **Chinatown Memoirs**

                              74 degrees and falling:

The current temperature of this illusion.

## Slick Gus & His Cranky Aunt

                Television:
              Masturbation:
The nerve rending despondency
Of hunting a dead lion.

## The Foibles of Modern Architecture

                the moon astutter

                thus to creep with her mercuries of echol
                                                      ali
                                                                 a
                              divides the moods of
night
                                                   into   streams   of
frailty
                                        then a final simpering
        n      o      i          t              a
        r      o              p                            a
        v
                e:
                          all darkness who beckons to swelling
                the mother through her intricacies of womb
                        plays one last immotile hush
                        on the fadeless thread
                        where no distance is breached
                        & no shade falters:
I would, that thine own pale sleeket
                        immateriality
  never come to rush or exclamation
                    but slip in & outwardly
                                through
the thoroughfares of shoosh and bedlamlessness
              above these cities of bruised
     and frozen steel
till there is not an eye left
pandering
                      reverence to porcelain
   till there is not a tide to sluice beneath
your gravity.

## **Thirty Years Till Birth**

       Here we cross the bridge of a falling star
As a child runs his fingers through the water;

Here our ancestors speak in silhouette;
       Here your skin is the color of the clay
       They would mend with their hands
To form the deities their children prayed to
       Before they slept.

Here you part your hands like scriptures of this clay.

Here the mural of your body will unweave itself
       & a diamond of plasma will fulminate
Through the scarlet history
       Of your toenails.

              Here the Gods are our servants—
              We fashion them from the clay
       & pull them from each other's ribs.

Here the fragrance of jasmine
Translates into indigo,
Mingles with sulfur
In the shallow marshes of a nova,
The belly of a meteor,
       In a eucharist of pollen;
A holy efflorescence and insemination
       That opens the eyes of our blood
       As it closes its mouth
       Inside us.

## The Berlin Wall Is Alive & Well & Living in Paris

    Revel in the painted mirrors and the
roulette wheel fashions of sound:

        bottles of light:
    autocratic voices of suspense;
            the Magazine Pageant thresh:

—self-promoting
sacrament of sabbatical from the pharmacy—

    —meet me at the corner of Sacrilege and
Stain—
               (sabbath of neutered wings)

        ozone stammers like a looked-at child—
        thunder knees itself in
the ovaries—
        the fog disembowels,
            hearing the hot girl—
        the abyss goes blank in the
collapsing dove parchment of dawn—
cloud brokers dislodge under the didactic audit of…?

        tinctured murmur, insignificant rain—
           halos in a torch bed—
water idols illuminate their faces of borrowed
delicacy—
the saboteurs grated shadow flower
descries the kingdoms
        blushing as they merge.

## **Thanks for the Calculator**

We need to connect.

Take a step in the right direction.

I'm really concerned about your availability.

It's a trust issue.

I need you to take on this project.

We need to process through it

Then discuss further responsibility

Before we make

A decision.

## **Brazen Simpletons**

                                      neon     slogans.

            we are not as real
        as the almighty dollar
              bill. we are not
      as light as paper
        we are as
              weightless as stars.

            aurora borealis
      in the dance of micturation—

     the celestial sales clerk
            sins to supervise.

the godless heathens we were braying against
              were, in actuality,
        the gods we were worshipping
through our closed circuit sacraments.

comatose benediction
sideways from the worm moist
pink envelope of the preacher's mouth:

        summer toppled cartwheels
     in the songstorm from the organ keys
then cracked her spine on the rigid
      hypothesis cash string:
          the holy uniformity
      dauntlessly breaking the materials
            for beauty.

## **Don't Let Me Catch Your Mom Smiling At Me**

acid house production kit
slow worm ringleader
telescopic metronomes
*Frog Eagle landed here*
dapperdils and ladylacs
coriander symposium
turtle egg synthesis
pretty boy pervert positive
plutonium berries
Elder Barry's antelope
game shoe extract
cyanide fiberglass katydidn'ts
circadian fluid
Sylvester Stallone patrimony
new age inbred
nimble glass factory
laundry pill doldrums
shattered ice yields broken codes
sheep become more than gods
barnyard elitist
construction wielding cheap telephone cards
love seat shit
twenty dollar incline
dill pickle expert
thermometer lampoon
patriotic lovemuscle
patronizing lovegun
plebeian plutocrat
paralegal ass. degree
napalm gardener
Ralph Nader buffet
Land's End Avenue
neutral dietitian
clear-thinking cock-talker
lottery card code-walker
Kamchatka plesiosaurus

periodical patronimbus
tip jar follower
pterodactyl tiramisu
tawdry Tawny Kitaen
*any way you want it*
eclectic nihilist Exhibit A
icecapades adulteress
sulfuric tarot
Succotash Fitzgerald
kimono dragons
lip gloss caramel
it's slit rock and roll for honey
fumbled death pitch
*dealt extra time running wild*
afterlife experiment #99
attack of the ingrown platypus
introverted monsters and monoliths
mobsters dismantle classified skeleton
morbid self-impressionism
corpulent copromane conductor
memoirs of neurotic bacillus
Bacchus candy cyst and desist
compartmental mastermind
Dick Little, Dr. please

## **A Version of the Future Annexed**

wildboys on glistening wings
smoking hashish
listen through the trees
cars explode in the street
birds with radios
sculpted to their throats
sing:
    *calamity*
preachers doused in kerosene
versify the purses
of evangelical habitués
who will meet their ends
without deliverance
in the chapels
where every Sunday
they took the holy sacrament in vain

## **An End Without Ending**

born in Boston
the sensitive progeny of thespians
who too soon past
taken in by his uncle
though never adopted
sent to an academy in England
where he painted murals
on his dorm room walls
after he was discharged from the army
for insubordination he attended
the University of Virginia
then married his thirteen-year-old cousin of the same name
though her soul and many others like it
would be preserved in the epithet Annabel Lee
      as a man the world was not his stage
      it was an actress
shifting from curtain to portrait
      something deeper than G-d
      drove his pen
      through his mind

the pages he found as empty
as an after funeral hearse
the words he found as empty
as the Universe

      though we all must find our end
      let us pray it is not in the pages
      of the man named Edgar Allan Poe

## **Ending Without an End**

      At the thin line between twelve and two:
           Pale sheen tangles of lightning
           Matted against the black western sky;
           Plateaus like somnolent lions.
It is impossible here to escape the circuits of Time:
It wilts and manifests without cease;
It absolves and persecutes the same;
      Pages creased by my father's hands
      Form the stories I've titled with my name.
        Your story is one of corridors,
          Countless avenues merging in a knife;
Evacuating galaxies of mime and echo;
          A desolation of Anasazi film scores;
     The memory of a poem or the poem's memory:
You have imagined these things as I've shown them to you,
      Thus we've entered each other's stories,
      Creating a third story between us.

      This is our story's end.

## **An Ending Without End**

    Numberless are the things of the void:

       Are we to be the void
or simply of it?

# Chem Trails

*The war goes on as long as you live,
the main thing is to stand on your own two feet.*

~Alfred Döblin

## **Pre**

The psychiatrists are here—
Count me in their number.

## **Pep Rally**

Hello,
I am Mr. Collier
Behind my eyes there is a mask
Laughing at you.
Remind me why
Conventional?
I've been accused
Of wanting to restore vitality to poetry.
Will you give these goddamn mummies their
                insurance premiums?

I am proud to announce
That you will all one day
Be kissing my ass or
Be wrong.
Don't worry too much, though,
I am, as you say, just a lowbrow comedian and
You still have twenty years
To die.

Steven Jesse Bernstein.
Roberto Bolaño.
Jack Kerouac. Beckett.
They're with me on this one:
Fuck You.

Do you know that you're secretly irrelevant?

## T

Testosterone climbed through your window
        looking for a job of work.
You postulated an apple in his diaper
        so he flagged down Winter Soldier
and they performed a nativity
        on your bathroom floor.
Now Winter Soldier's got a mammoth
        predilection
    for the exercise machine in the foyer
and won't take no for an answer
        nor lift a finger
    when it comes to house chores.
Testosterone is curled up
        like a marble faun
            in a mirror of perfumed frost
        with dishes still to do
    and sinks to scrub.

## **Capsule**

My mom was a closed system.
My mom was without a pretty idea.
My mom loved partially at eighteen
Searching for the film
With a stranger.
I gave her the courage to provide
So I've never wondered
Who at the office
Was guest singing.

She could do her best
To save
And soon some man would take it.
Somewhere there's a girl
Chained to her favorite abortion.
My freedom takes its place
Naked on my soul's lips:
A multitude of tigers
With their fingers at each other's breasts.

My mom was etched in a cup
And I told her
*Tears are never enough,*
I told her as I left her.

## **Admiralty**

infertile theater of asphalt and stars
producing dawn

## **Postpartum Postmortem**

My name is Prayer Bead.
I have engaged the gold baton
from my foster mother's navel
once more to snap the champion's tape
with my belly button.

I forgive you.
Kiss my class ring.
I have a gift for your cholesterol
(the 401K decathlon victor
offers a vivisectomy
shadow show for your troupe):

Make Addiction scrub the toilets after supper,
wash the car windows at the gas station
and bathe the dogs;
you have holidays to accrue
and doctors to usurp
through casual chess games.
In every can of body cream
A dozen Nefertiti's wait to go to work.

Looks mean nothing
but you must look better than all
or lose your eyes and wrists.
In every tube of spermicide
a night of drinking will occur,
not so much the inverse.
Take heed if you value your life
and fear breast milk.

A forest is a city waiting to erect:
Learn this before you tan your loin cloth.

Water fondles all it touches.
Be like water in a business suit
or lacrosse shorts.

### *!!!Quinten Collier!!!*

Franz Kafka was this chick I used to date—
        humorless, opaque, malnourished, clingy,
  systematically jealous to boot—
she always forgot to flush the toilet
        and made ham sandwiches that tasted like sand,
  complaining all day about her mother.

Her skin was like varnished pink Saran Wrap.

She had a down home insignificance about her
        and was always getting misplaced or lost,
  locked in port-a-johns at White Snake concerts,
    shoved down flights of stairs by novice nurse maids,
  diddled by college professors and featherweight pimps—
      I think that about sums up our first date.

The sex change came as no surprise
  —some souls just get put into the wrong body—
but when she told me the name she'd picked,
      I admit, I laughed in her face.

            !!!QUINTEN COLLIER!!!

Sounds like a fashion catalog
      or an Alaskan fish wizard—

Why not Sappho or Ayn Rand or
        Edna St. Vincent Millay?
      Something bespeaking dignity and station,
not a name that conjures up scummy one nighters
        in scabbed-out restaurant sinks...

!!!QUINTEN COLLIER!!!

            *!!!QUINTEN COLLIER!!!*

At least they'll have the courage to kill themselves.

## **Vengeance of the Dream World:**

I have lost all instinct towards Beauty.
Gravity is like a five-hundred-pound stockbroker
Turning into a waterfall.
The mother with the crack pipe
Is beyond all illusion.
White obsidian:
Somewhere the bees are infested with it;
They'll wipe our minds clean
And they are only make believe:
Having once been children...
Ticks and flees don't kill the dog
But their diseases certainly do.
Tomorrow is infected with illustrations
That turn divine as we erase them.
O the lily in the bed pan
Wilts into a heart
Beyond all illumination.
It is the Sphinx who pisses in cuneiform,
Her gonorrhea a radioactive litter box crossword,
A glow-in-the-dark Ibis speaking ex natura rei.
"I will come back for you," she says,
"Provided Emptiness insists
And M/mercury is still your favorite color."

### **No One's Ark**

I have squandered the beasts of the Earth
And must remake them.
It is enough.
Otter, platypus, snake & dove;
Zebra, porcupine, elk & dog:
Once you were only photographs,
Now you are only words.

## **Barges**

      Shipyard is the director of this program—
Her doughnut is getting cold.
          She tells the lights to shut up
      then caresses the espionage
        and mutual aid button.
I wouldn't ask her for a raise just yet,
           better wait
       till the tendons thaw
and the contestants have all been
            electrocuted.

Cue camera 2.

## **Air Cysts**

      Existence is landing!

      Come down from your tableaus! Reduced prices!

Start quitting today!

Decide now:
         Somewhere in me
      The monster is a sphere
         Enantiomorphing
    And the courts should be called to court!

          NNNAAAAHHHH!!!

Impalpable?

    Sing for the listening
    Unlistened to!
    Sing Sunday Norman Rockwell
    Normal rock winner!
    People deserve to live next door to you!
    You owe it to own it!
    Rickety Tooth
    Runt's Congested
    Bipolar Vulgus!
    Americana Quietude
    Hamstring Platter!
    To Hell on a half-diet!

Can I take a marriage?

      In 6 months you will hold a job!

    Free sofa!

    Believe Sheep Dog is good in life?
    His room is sharing a pick-up mistress

With Comfort Book's beer voice!

*Respondez!*
*Respondez!*

Everything will be read aloud
Then uneverything penalized with tap dance!

I am sending my choice to you.
Will you clean it?
Why nasal nurture the soporific?
Wet incredulous I goiter. *Toupee!*

Red Spa!
Red Spa!

Communist measles need kinderhaus!

Onion corset!
She is buxom slim slum-Muslim
Voltaic advantageously!
Her name is Drug Clinic
And I am Thin.
I do have Can't
Cantilevered against her salve,
Her lampshade meant,
Unctuous enter I through nine months
Eternity,
The first to see the roving stars
For lice,
I am spending my joist,
Axle crooked so exfigure
Also
Emporium trumpets
And dust to dust to dust.

Nothing is lost
That can't be lost.

## El Topo II

The sunlight turned to smoke above the desert.
The caravan wound westward
In search of the naked thighs of mice.
A Russian gypsy named Takato Yamamoto.

The sunlight turned to dust above the mountain.
The caravan wound westward.
A Russian gypsy married to his mother
In a mask of self-hypnosis.

The sunlight turned to soot under the horse hooves.
Takato Yamamoto
In search of the everlasting serpent.
A puppeteer in a mask of human muscle.

A gunslinger, a pedophile,
And a Russian,
Crawling behind a miracle,
Turned to sunlight.

The sunlight turned to Takato Yamamoto in the fountain,
Muscle memory:
*I appear terrifying. Fear Evil
And everlasting life,* said the serpent.

The gypsy turned to ashes in the sunlight.
*The mice have found her.
The caravan is now our mother,
We cannot be born.*

The puppeteer shot a child in the sunlight.
*We are not alive:
That is what draws us to the womb.
My name is Takato Yamamoto, the Blessed Serpent.*

*Only the mice are everlasting.*

The gunslinger with a mask made of horse hooves.
Westward wound the caravan.

The snake's crypt of sunlight.

## **Noah's Ark**

I remember
Scarlett fever
As my escort
To the cave where
Eagles, dolphins,

(follow me down
to the seashore:
pony, plaster,
salve and sweet gum;
let me show you
Daddy's trophy

[Mother Meadow
Wept alone
In the room where
Shadows will come]

water spigot
shined and foaming)

Lions, horses,
Cracked like winter
With forgiveness.

## **Sade**

I no longer get excited.
I never charge the stage
to throw my panties at the guitarist
or hang my bra from the candelabra.

It's castor oil,
the whip,
or the closet with rats

until the baby dies.

## After Work

it is best to worship
exclusively at the table
when dinner is served
and the day has been consequenced;
when the assembly line
images newscast and impotent
dress shirts are draped
over the backs of chairs
as if they have been seen
then it is time to call upon our___.

## Infra-Dada Manifesto

Receive the ordinance.
Give back your property.
Tend to the flock.
Make the child a cerebral mess.
A rolling spore gathers no moss.
I believe all illness should be cured
With Amoxicillin.
Flash of lightning over the prairie just like
A light bulb popping in a plastic bag.
Enjoy the wirtschaftswunder.
Pro-proletariat.
First round #1 draft pick:
Retired.
Beautiful spoon red as sunset:
Expired.
Drunk sex-offender dishwasher:
Rehired.
Bring me The Tea Party.
Yes, Comandante Top Zero.
Sub-Prime Mortgage Prime Rib
Prime Minister,
Minestrone, Pasta Primavera:
Inculcate me that Chimera.
Citadel: civilian crystal
Plaza where they pump the student
Body full of steroids.
Is my salad ready?
Organic as milktoast,
Blood pudding.
We have the plum mediocre
On a supplemental program;
We replace the heart with an orange:
Citric bypass.
It makes a good breakfast
For the masses pledging mop & sickle
To me: Herr Uber-Munch,

Mr. Normal Gospel Pornographer,
Fear Sommelier, Polaris General,
Emperor of the Common Good.
It's all so revolting.
The waiter won't be tipped.
You have my word:
George Washington.

## **Leper Friends**

My voice reaches for your cervix
I am a macrobiotic obstetrician
To teach you all the things about yourself
You could only learn from someone else

The melodies in your heart
Act like criminals
There is no way out
Of the methadone clinic

She delivers an orchid
That's how we spit 'em
Imbalanced
State pen

Disquiet in the home
Devouring and gracious
The Word is Delicatessen
As we're depicted

Grandma surprises cribbage
Crank up the remission
The everlasting light
In search of cowardice

You're a good doctor
You're a dull instrument
The reactor's
Tears and essence

That's how we spin 'em
Our Lady of Grief
Democracy, AIDS, kitten,
What will we become?

There's so much about myself
When she's catatonic
I could learn from someone else
Twilight

Mediocritic
Enough suffices
Water
Weaves

Our bodies' gospel
Penance is sin
Act
Mel

Sad Day
Adrenaline
Tranquilizers
I'm sermonizing again

Insignificant indifferent
Philosophies into one
Indelicate record of the ocean
Dissolves on your tongue

This is who we will become
The kiss's ass
Plagiarism
Volcanic stone

Mistresses
Antibiotic Street
Gang fuck
Vision trade

## **Civilianized**

They sent him to Afghanistan
    where he contracted
        hemorrhoids
  so they shipped him back
        to his couch
    and thus far
        it all proved
      unnecessary.

## **College**

Happy are you
Little spoon with chlamydia,
Today you can go back to school.
College is grand
At a breathtaking laundromat
And the Midwest extends her spatula.
It takes decades to dye
A cloud with repellant
Mosquito or elephantine;
Glissade Iridescence
Was the father of my nephew
Who died in the war from his tongue.
Now that you've learned
Oklahoma inconsequence
Should be a shoulder and burden ignored
Of I too so up in
Massachusetts with Kerouac
Thoreau cigarettes in my home.
The cut rate green sunsets
I park in my trailer
Pathological, saturnine;
I woke up unliving,
Trivial as exile
And drunk as a firefly
With the beach front lawn chairs
Contaminated with Knoxville
Raping themselves like sorority brides.
Gangrene gingivitis:
Wine from the gums;
A+ for the first one to cry.

## Growing Up in a Deodorant Factory with a Pen Pal in Tokyo

Oft times when I'm writing
I have no interest in what I'm writing.
Twelve years ago I was beginning an article,
Something like, "A Person Does Not Choose
Or Ways in Which We Learn the Usefulness of Deceit."
I lost direction before I began.
I stared at the ceiling.
I spayed a cucumber.
I pranked my carburetor.
I bathed my bag balm.
I watched aphids
Garden a blow up doll.

Nothing worked.

I picked up the phone and dialed Honeybee,
My most trusted friend and confidant.

"Honeybee?"
"You tastin' my stinger, right? Ain't it strange?"
"I need you to come over. We should take some pills."
"Honeybee's dead. This is her replacement, Golden Dog."
"Golden Dog! But I'm not supposed to talk to you.
I'm on punishment."
"Punishment? You're a grown-ass man."

I realized that the words of Golden Dog were true:
I was over 21, white and American.
Then I thought about my future, the future of all men.
I hung up the phone, snatched my pen,
and jotted down a title:
"Growing Up in a Deodorant Factory with a Pen Pal in Tokyo."
It would be the only article I would finish in my life.

I would like to dedicate this article to Golden Dog
PO Box !@#, Gap Fluctuation, CO 81501-10518

## **Mario Santiago**

I am looking for my doctor in an office building with ovular windows, pink bricks and escalators. I find a seat on the second floor. I realize the man sitting next to me is Mario Santiago. He looks like the bus driver from *City of God*: tall, lean and tan, with a large fro. We talk. He is amiable and describes for me an episode of astral projection—the product of LSD and self-hypnosis— then asks if I've ever had the desire to watch mothers and children burn. "It's all there is for people like us." After this we discuss Roberto Bolaño. We both agree he died too soon. Mario laughs until he coughs, canceling his appointment.

## **Ulysses (for Travis Flynn)**

I wonder if in a previous life
I was asked explicitly to bear this burden?
Even so, I know I would have said *Yes*,
Fearing otherwise to be made out a coward.

And that is that,
And the answer doesn't matter,
Thus I accept
This menial poison.

Ulises Lima
I am crying for you.
Broken poets
Give up.
There is no transcendence,
Just histories of crashed couches
On continents
We reach as we depart.

And the soul cannot be fabricated,
Though try we must.

## **Popsicle Aquifer**

Wipe the saliva off the sky,
My forehead desires it.
I am sweating in a coffin
Sweet as a lyre.
This decadent polyester balloon candy
Entices me.
Automatic sugar
Diabetes moonbeam
Slash eulogy seduces me,
Slipping off like stockings
Silky as an ear drum
Beating itself
To pulp in a seashell.
I will find my demise
In a basket of grapes,
Plums, pears & bananas.
Prepare the marmalade.
Men, I am here,
Distended as fruit cake,
Peanut butter.

## Fukushima

Behind the future
The glowing mouth
The atoms fold
A scar out of light
The vision a uterus
Where the fetus erodes
Like an engineer borne
Through a dying reactor

We dance like skeletons
Convinced they are children

The masks and the miracle
The paradox
The puzzled
Helix that coughs
In the face of its double

Flowering insects
Fission, fusion
Magnetic rain

The moonlight is human

The silhouette draws you
Like a pole draws a compass
You touch its skin

Concrete
Codex
Reduction

## **Don Juan in Hell**

does anybody know who allison is bought by the billionaire
    wife bought and paid for having his baby the heir
    traitor's heir you belong to me
lone star lawman high meadow master of horses in charge her
    lord protector captive splendor magic obsession
texas fury showdown texas passion the comeback cowboy
    bedded by the boss the boss's baby bargain
the hellion bride the spanish bride the prince's texas bride take
    no prisoners
truly madly manhattan one daddy too many the cradle will fall
    a rogue's promise
all i desire stranded with santa a cold day for murder
love me only autumn lover imagine love once upon a rose
    dark prince
seduced by the enemy beloved enemy phantom lover let's
    pretend the husband test two weeks with a stranger
the other side of midnight acts of love where shadows go no
    one heard her scream slightly sinful slightly tempted
    the blooding never love a stranger
skin deep something wicked call no man father a wolf in
    sheep's clothing quinn's inheritance
the heiress bride expecting brand's baby love's gentle journey
    doorstep daddy father in the middle
the calhoun women: lilah and suzanna the sherbrooke bride
    tame the wind the wild winds dance upon the air storm
    tide dream tide heaven and earth
sweet talk rogue river frontier women love me only the
    calhoun women: catherine and amanda the loner the
    forbidden bride my lady beloved the oldest virgin in
    oakdale mackenzie country
on the way to the wedding a woman of virtue to have and to
    hold taming natasha the scottish bride luke's runaway
    bride the trapper the romantic lady lyte's little secret
    smokescreen marriage
butterfly are you lonesome tonight miss merridew's flowers
    falling for the doctor only in my dreams plain jane

gypsy lover secrets of the heart after the kiss waiting
for nick fortune hunter's hero
midnight touch cordina's crown jewel secret touch the bad
place longarm on the goodnight trail chase wheeler's
woman harrigan's bride night shield chill factor
hot ice silver bells coming back alive hell hath no fury the
cowboy first lady a tender loving iron lace
heartbreaker educating gina the bodyguard the stone
flower garden angel a warrior's lady
the maccaferty's slade the greek bridegroom passion's pawn
desert rogue falcon's desire
a scandalous marriage love's desperate deceit the seduction
one night for love christmas eve wedding reckless
endangerment the heart has no voice
demons pass the wings of morning the silver rose kingdom of
moonlight
jack and jill inner harbor toxic bachelors catch a wild heart
mr. montgomery's quest kiss me kaitlyn love me tomorrow
irish hearts rivals and lovers
life with riley romancing the crown cinderella's convenient
husband more than meets the eye diamonds and desire
the asking price

**Marilyn Manson**

I'm in an elevator with Marilyn Manson. He's wearing combat boots, black jeans, black Marilyn Manson t-shirt, a black denim jacket and a black ball cap. His hair is shorter than usual, reaching just below the ears. He says if I suck his dick I'll unlock the secret of the universe. Down go his pants and out pops his cock, 30% erect, fat and red. I take it in my mouth, trying to talk myself into enjoying it. He never gets hard.

We are in some half-decimated office building, part of the underground resistance. Outside the world is coming apart. Beyond the window the ruins of a stone structure, like an ancient Greek temple, disgorge themselves onto the street. Below, our comrades are waiting for us, fleeing from the police who no longer exist: we run from nothing now because we're so used to running.

## **Leonard Cohen, Spy**

Today Leonard Cohen is on set. He plays a spy constantly seducing beautiful women. The backdrop is a giant liquid zoetrope. He seems affable, embracing the unknown as a known commodity. He's not going to be happy when I tell him we're shooting a commercial.

## Amortization Ampere-Hour

I am head of the Sepia Tone Committee.
Do you think sunlight too brittle?
Memory too derivative?
Time incapable of being sustained?
It can't go on like this.
You must see the old photograph and learn the truth.
Join us in our lobby for the grand unveiling.
Pre-emptive nostalgia—
The supreme Art Official—
Blowing nicotine through canvas curtains.
Autumn gives the best testamonies.

Lunging through the smoke at the terminal
(each star erased by the
white-blue sky
a cataract or drop of bleach).

You will receive your assignment.

## **Ammonia**

The astral union:
Buddha finds perfection through
drinking his own piss.

## The Beetle Leg

catchers gate valve
manifolds, plug valve
manifolds, inspected
and recertified flow iron
hydrostatic tested all equipment.

Serviced accumulators
and flow back equipment.

I did frac water management
for Halliburton.

I was shop supervisor
at professional wireline
and rentals in Louisiana
until new general manager
brought his own people.

I was crew leader
for crown supply co.
in Colorado.

Roustabout work on oxy
assembling, rebuilding,
inspecting, testing
frac production equipment.

Pinning, inspecting
9 5/8 casing hangers
and inspecting
4 inch hangers.

Occasionally going to
the field and installing frac
production equipment.

I worked at cameron
in the production department
visually inspecting, repairing,
testing, greasing frac equipment
to be shipped to other facilities,
ensured daily quota was met
in a timely manner
and all employees time working
managed efficiently.

## **Manifesto of the Youth Brigade**

12-year-old products of youth detention facilities trained in the
 use of tasers and batons;
Assembly line facade boys and girls for night patrol;
16-year-old ministers of information retrieved from inner city
 slums;
Every skin tone and ethnicity represented by the Military
 Industrial Complex:
We are present.
For this purpose our heritage distinguishes us.
We serve to protect our country as it is our property, as it
 serves to protects us;
The station hunting;
Anyone who exhibits behavior we must protect from those
 around us who protect us from those who exhibit;
Our plan, our future.
We are the correct candidates,
Our privilege correct.
We confront the challenges before us, the task at hand;
It is a burden we confront to have no choice but to confront;
We are not rewarded for our efforts: we receive an order;
Many of us are ready;
Many of us have the courage.
We are aware it will take unmitigated sacrifice.

We are trained in the martial arts and all other techniques of
 hand to hand combat.
The statutes of our protocol:
We march in rank through the school halls and shopping
 plazas.
We have been trained to kill:
We cannot fail.

## Other Green Stars

soon Mary soon
the lavender shell
edging the moon
will unhinge

the balance
this eclipse
this ride
my last ticket

I have the bitter bone
I don't belong
I have
it's pearling

not one last excuse
that must be
atoms
that taste

and now it is
singed
wallpaper expires
in all directions

in the mouth
in all directions
the fetid compass
of her fingers

the dwarf stars
Mary
do you believe
you remember

Uranus twilight

you asked me
beneath the bells
in her mouth

in all directions
you remember
you believe
in twilight

this is my ticket
the dwarf stars
the balance
the eclipse

the bitter bone
that sways
I have
you asked me

the subtitle
cigarette
zodiac margin
the blinds that must be closed

lavender margin
the quintessence of
the blinds
that must be closed

Mary
in the chatter
shedding their winter coats
and opening

a zodiac of gas masks
the water
punctuates us
as orbits

the flood
is folding
back
I am leaving

the window in the glass
glowing
on the symmetrical
window in the glass

I am leaving Mary
this is my ticket
it is impossible
to be free

the balance
before the moment of the balance
annihilates
the moment

we are boundless
I annihilate the moment of myself
to maintain
the balance

the last
glass cigarette
isotopes
the dwarf stars in her fingers

in all directions
you remember
you believe
and must be closed

## **Gravity Lane**

The future for them now is the future for you:
Surrounding tissue stretched to the limits;
The focus closes in on her;
Some hidden personal wreckage rotates to her right to the
        face;
Clients as soon as she has taken a step into the reverse;
Quickly turning bronze the stairs to the right:
We have for viewing today windows on the back wall the sun
        a nice new model out;
Pop up:
Entryway into a large empty space practiced as she begins;
Fingers like opening the door rotating back to her face of gray
        tile;
Carpet ash extends up the stairs;
The human eye vibrant manufactured retracting energy filter
        denuded as white walls;
Introduction portfolio three bedrooms of paper;
Second floor to the left she faces her clients;
As is the kitchen separated from the living room;
Off the back wall ceilings everything in the house passes
        through the white blind dust the eye;
Contact with her clients:
Counter stem imperceptible with their two pallid single family
        formed through the same door;
White front home with more human white front door;
Two story blue vinyl facade the real estate agent front lawn
        knee-high white vinyl fence by a varicose wall;
White leather blonde;
Sync view:
Your average some impossible stands under the front door
        awning on her face white paper glinting expertly in the
        sun two eyes grin with caps not breaking;
Commercially vibrant business painted on her face we enter
        there's not much to say about anyone;
In her early fifties boxed in beaming infertile the chirp not
        threatening the slender entryway to her left;

Formica handle with her manicure belying a two car garage
    three bedroom two bath innocuous expanding onto
    the piqued living room;
Unobtrusive chipper here we have safety inexistence complete
    the spaces between the doors;
Turn on play click when syncing first letter this one is no
    different gray concrete smooth and complicated;
The scene dissolves leaning against the rail at the bottom of
    the stairs;
To serve no impediment if no one were so inclined;
Tool chests a small boat a motorcycle a deep freeze door on
    electric track a dog kennel value from ideas at the
    service of your ideas;
Without averting her gaze from her clients we'll take care of
    the details;
Once again reconstitutes the team an excellent wall
    here we are as we pass up the stairs you get quality
    that cares living outstanding results;
We make it happen first letters in tape we're the best when you
    work with us wearing her vacuous smile internal abyss
    as she starts speaks then starts;
Guaranteed in the business we build our lives with the lives
    we build number the materials re-sync add dash the
    summit unravels into some as the rest of the house
    terminating in a window;
Here we have safety for the loved ones one client
    three bedrooms two baths on the top floor at a time;
The tread of tires room enough for two cars or one pictures of
    the tread of tires the upper level hallway sinks into her
    with two doors on the top step fiberboard vinyl plaster;
Skimming over outstanding agents with love as we pass
    positioned precisely for five star service;
Enough homes for hanging up pictures the upper level hallway
    of the ones on each side floating symmetrically in a
    haze of the ideas and vitality;
Rises all is still the first and last time we didn't see each other
    in the hall is as banal and vacant but for our traces;
The top now seems destined for prints of equivocal aspects we

have a splendid neutral hallway here;
Accommodate what is done insert new entries landscapes she seems to think what we can do for you;
Bathroom steps into the inside a sunless box a closet door with a last flashing locked in;
Recover her exterior of ordinary size window door to her left to her right she opens the first door having heard so much when the age comes up the stairs and into this room out of the car through the front door;
How to operate a sink or a tub you drag the door to the hall down the highway into the car telling them together we make a great team;
At making more possible opens the bathroom door from the bedroom and enters now in a mechanical voice and movement you could put babies or an office in here the window blinded on her right the door to the bathroom;
Suddenly this is the service you deserve then emptied every day the bathroom skeleton and speak;
Such institutions they forget how to walk they can no longer drive but you want to make sure their diaper bag is blank the whole time from the people you trust;
The bathroom nobody does it better your days excrement exfoliating the residue of immotile expanses and you apply make up crop stubble pine floor cabinet linoleum which ends;
This is the smaller of the three bedrooms spent now expect the best faucet and basin mother and father tub and shower for dripping should be placed ten by ten;
Excrement the mirror rinsed and cropped stubble tartar where you think what we can do for you for toiletries where you expel from hands the power tools to buy a home;
Commode going through the motions in defeat leave excrement in plaque and burst pimples behind in states of deterioration over which the rug the people trust nursing hushed here's the closet door devoid of movement;
Their own senile and incontinent might say or eat with a hose

down their throat;
One quiescence about to stale unimposing locking;
Don't change scan back in and click complete exit into the
   hallway without her clients paying cutting directly to
   the facing door opens it and enters a large room as she
   turns to face her clients does so a ghost of sunlight
   peters in making us feel parched;
Uneasy to illumine you live at the humorless seldom the days
   union of vigil and lips of one as the other common
   doggedly purblind dreams of found and hidden paces
   over to the closet slides open the door points to the
   door on the opposite wall until the desire;
This mundane autumn find ourselves is repealed unutterable
   here in the mommy and daddy pulls open the last
   blanched leaf rendered undressing stands on the
   threshold;
Perform to passion paralysis a real uncommon wisdom alone
   in space where the money lives most likely while her
   pictures and old letters left as sterile as big as the first
   room the door to the bathroom to her right staring
   within us;
Of the last prayer of the one suffocating we value your time
   and zeal a double sliding door for a closet on two large
   windows less ineffectual now before;
Tedium the unrestrained room we've opened the door to less
   each night wasted the master closet pleasuring for
   garments and shoes;
Baldness into the same baldness by anyone but you and us;
From the right a washer and drier to the garage and in your life
   she has been struck as if you were out there with them
   just as the terror came she recovers herself making
   every moment more natural anything is possible it is as
   if that is why there is a window on the other end;
The things you don't want seen paying no attention to her
   clients struck by the unnatural each other we're now in
   the master bedroom as gasping to see the same thing as
   before;
Here's the master bathroom between the few blank

expressions I showed you the weapons I don't want to
have disappear will unlearn the thrill but on a larger
scale;

Amnesia of the thrill is too dim with less of your bowels
purgatory to waft out the last door you can open this
one comes with a window slit the blinds spy on
yourself so we the neighbors where in the hours
inescapable looking into herself but it is pitch black;

Exits back into the hall does not enter heeding the memory as
if stricken slumbers in the destitute stench or the event;

Here today across the living room from the world outside a
slight tremor her eyes it's time for an expert those of
one lost by two wicker chairs;

Doors now open in the left corner a door contains steps with a
slightly tarnished aura now her ocular link to her
clients her poise ebullience;

Sashays a coffee table once again without losing into the
kitchen a bookcase the TV and entertainment center
very spacious very comfortable;

Transcription sync now onto the garage let's move onto the
wonderful kitchen which includes all the essential
space you need when cooking and cleaning to have the
life you want as soon as it passes as if you'd never
even set foot there;

As soon as she steps foot into the kitchen it is as if she pauses
briefly an uninspiring affair;

Dining room with tiles the same hue as the carpet perfect for a
couch wall mounted though the lapse leaves her and
the pantry;

Even the kids in the back here tomorrow twin recliners
a dog kennel isolated for memorabilia the place where
you can relax and;

You get all the natural light scurries to the other end of the
kitchen steps through the door opens the door to the
garage now here we have the living room a window in
the walls on either end some inexplicable fear passing
through her for breakfast and lunch insert tape number;

We're embracing ingenuity come out here's some malignant

       premonition she has let guard her invoice daily
          update print and fill out;
Everyday you need to know to eat try the touch of the smile
          that makes everything much simpler standing before
          her in there;
In notes check completed pay a stove and fridge a sink and a
          dish machine the stove and fridge the sink the dish
          machine the washer and drier;
Cupboards counters with cupboards underneath doors a back
          room defined by the kitchen;
You'll be moving in without you say and you not knowing
          the tense the pulse whatever makes you happy that
          shouldn't this is not she forces no plan of moving what
          could be and you have;
Never losing sight of her clients so you can watch as her tone
          has changed sprightly regaining this end is the fantastic
          for a dinner table and her demeanor;
You already live here in there for the son and daughter the
          dogs the final room you come out raises her head to
          find her clients staying in the place you are how do you;
So when can we expect how long do you plan and here is the
          ruffle of curtains her eyes brighten the right
          relationship is everything every time you ask how can
          we help you;

## Woody Allen

My wife and I have attended a cocktail party at Woody Allen's. We're the last guests to leave. He and his wife—Diane Keaton—are seeing us off, making small talk on the foyer. Woody asks me again what it is I do. I answer—without any ulterior motive—that I am currently at work on a play. This instantly discomfits him. He starts stammering. Obviously, he thinks I'm going to ask him to read it. With brisk formality he ushers us out the door, saying, "We'll have to get together soon. Maybe we can play with dolls." I take the last remark as an insult, until I notice Woody has a hard-on. I look away as my wife guides me backwards through the door, both of us pretending to laugh as Diane overcompensates with good nature to save face. On a small chestnut table with long curling wrought iron legs I notice four flowerless stems protruding from a matte black vase.

Out in the street we hail a cab. We ride through an endless shanty town, the plywood and cardboard hovels graffitied in vivid colors. A purple mist circulates around the neon characters and icons, drawing a viridescent steam out of them, commingling with it, though the miniscule pixels of the twinned vapors remain completely individuated from one another. "So this is what it's like to be poor," my wife says as if the words revealed themselves to her only after they were spoken. I look at her, a reflection of the woman I cannot seem to find.

Our destination is a dream: we are living in a forest ranger's cabin in the desert, the caretakers of ancient cliff dwellings where an ant-sized people thrived eons ago. A huge transparent purple and green python floats down the path at dusk. My wife follows him, convinced that he is harmless, or that life is meaningless: either way, I recognize she is locked in his spell. I follow them beyond the cliff dwellings, to a pool where the sound of an extinct waterfall can still be heard. I must remove all thoughts of shelter from my mind to regain her, to relive a symbiosis that is always vanishing.

## **Occupations of the Elite**

The exhausted, amoral
psychic
vigilante.
Naked eunuch
salad bearer.
Rifle owning
frequenter of strip clubs
and gay parades.
Doxologists.

(This is the story of a species
   on the brink of collapse;
Alien governments
   cooperating with the CIA…
Where do you think babies come from?)

(This is the story of a species
   on the brink of consecration;
The aspirant, ascendant, phlegmatic,
   Antiherophilus assimilated by a baser law,
cavorting the studied and principled hedonism
   of demi-escorts
who live forever with each discarded munition;
   frottage of stars, attar of cheap roses,
expensive silhouettes, isonomy,
   psychogenic retrograde clairaudience;
      to hold, to violate, to suppress;
   the same pristine light longed for by instaforms;
      every shadow commanded to need,
dependent in duplicity and parallelity,
      with the sole objective to search
for flesh to reflect itself in
   without searching;)

Truncated Byron
dining on

Jove.

(This is the story of a species
 on the brink of concentration;
sending pictures of leaked wombs,
 open muscles;
every living being immolated;
 nothing divulged;
fear that can't be purged;
 squeaky-clean pleiotaxis;
 lying to each other,
ignoring each other;
 vast fields of raw buttocks
undulating;
 wet lip-colored knots
cringing in the morbid sinew of a liberated mithridate
 preview application:
the Big Bang never ends:

## The Anti-Teatre

He was a greaser—a total impostor who attached himself with all the other detritus that spring. His first performance was to be called *The Donkey*. We set him up in the basement of an evacuated school.. The room was packed wall to wall with all kinds of stereo equipment, kitchen appliances, furniture, decorations, etcetera: the waste of a thousand failed yard sales tossed haphazardly into a pyre. A half-assed spray-painted banner clung to the ceiling. The kid was convinced we believed in him, that this would be his breakout performance, shattering all former notions of theatre and its consequences. The audience and troupe members stumbled around the junk pile. The room was kinetic with anticipation—at least two different varieties. We patted our pupil on his back and plied him with assurances worthy of our trade as we made sure his partner for the performance never arrived. He told us—when it became undeniable that he would be making his debut alone—the lack of accompaniment would only make the piece stronger—"more severe" was his phrase. Due to the high level of expectation, he felt obligated to go on before he had totalized the new solo dynamic in his head. At first the performance went well. He was the Donkey with a master who never materialized, putting his character into the strange predicament of having to guide itself with the rope tied around its neck. Our actor walked on his hands with his back to the ground, sliding up a slanted filing cabinet, crawling across plastic totes; he toppled sideways through paper debris and coffee machines. Initially the behavior seemed authentic: a perfect mime, in fact: an astute commentary on the power manifest by the individual's need to be suppressed; but as his finger was caught in the hinge of a metal folding chair our hero broke. The audience can forgive one breech, but as the youth continued to clamor, to stumble in the manner not of the character, but of himself, the crowd's patience wore thin. Soon, he was operating exclusively under the pretext of their good humor, struggling to salvage at least some minor portion of the reality he'd failed to inhabit.

## **Self-Sacrifice Superslut**

I died of starvation perfected G-d's suicide tickle ejaculated myself back into the viremia through the desert with a bottle of perfumed bullshit and cavities and widows stark and naked and spayed as ghosts.

## **Nazi Literature in the Americas**

I am on my way to Hitler.
He is maneuvering my enemies
Like cloisonné guns
With new pawn certificates.
*Now it is okay to be bad,* he says.

These are my friends:
They ennoble my pornography addiction
Before a jury of loculicidal sex stars,
Hyenas and girls that pass me by.

*I want to fuck a witch trial,* I say,
*If you're not going to put out—*
*Even if you are.* I want the Final Show.
The insoluble spadix
That will leave me unpinned,
All meaning
And magnetic poles.

*But you have seen the Final Show,* he says,
*And all you did was complain.*

*No one arrives.*

## The USO

Lesbian panther
throwing a farewell party
for scalage.
Confetti executive
dreaming of cleaning
a war desk.
Larval Thyiad
pulling the moonlight off her face
into her panties.
Venerable surgeon
with pink cloven-hoof
implants.
Venal trustee
sitting in
her husband's
shit.
Venereal student
at the grape
at the sun's tip.
Humiliated newborn
with feathers.
Buxom software engineer
exhuming her sarcophagus of
God-eaten vizards.
Sly polo scholar
with underlings
digressive
in taste and scent
collapsing into rage
for epochs
with his parents' pure body
alternating in small doses
length and width,
lamp and candlelight.
Pathological Psyche

at the pool
with braided teeth.
In the dark loculus of Energy
the unfolded curio coordinator
escalates the snow so finely
men melt into opinions.
The cunning colloquial
silk moth,
a peacock in its mouth,
riding the dusk
like a vast diaphanous
accordion.
Soap magnate—
who cannot speak
without mentioning
how he cannot speak—
tossing a mutilated synapse
through a skim jealous
jalousie.

## **Terrorists**

Tomorrow's cancer
At yesterday's prices.

Optimal.
Deluxe.

Tomorrow's treatment:
Today's premiums.

Advancements in organized medicine
Have turned pregnancy into an illness:
In the next few years
We hope to cure it.

Let me tell you about the resistance:

## **Industrial Catacombs, Sacred Hardware**

I love it when they make the puppet talk.

I love to see the clothes his wife wears.

I love to congratulate myself on the color of his skin.

## Side Effects Include Preclusive Side Effects

Have you found yet the psychic absolute?
A device to allot perfect judgment?
The irremissible epiphany?
I have my formulas.
I obey my masters.
I do not seek mere perfection.
I want the non-referential
Emptiness with
An inherent lack of existence.
A natural radiance and
Resplendence will be simultaneously
Tolerated and abhorred.
Do you know who Samayatārā is?
The primordial Buddha Samantabhadra?
His consort Samantabhadrī?
I want to go to their orgy
To escape the contamination of
Inflamed flesh.

## **Cher**

On the co
bweb of he
r tongue I c
alcul
ate the los
s I coul
d have w
on.

## The DA/The Criminalization of Reality

This is the end of Gravity.
We can live forever
In a place that does not exist.
What does that mean,
*Living in the past?*
Ourselves the mirrors
That most resemble them.
Do we mostly resemble ourselves
Or do we?
When we look into ourselves
The heroes we hide
Show us their idols:
Artificial, complete,
Completely sterile
featuring The Sonic Dildo
By Patrick Carr.
Sugartime and Lucy
Were his disciplants.
They lived at the collective
With sybarite Jesus
From 2150 A.D.
They said,
*There's a scar on your face*
*For every sin you've committed*
*And two for every grace.*
*We found this answer*
*Searching in the wrong place.*
*We are our heroes' idols,*
I said.
*The art of leisure*
*Is the art of dying easily.*
*Do not be mislead,*
*Your time is not spent*
*Increasing.*

The hierophants magazined over the waters:
Cognizance and wax.

## Death Trip 2015

Dragrace in the desert
Death Trip
70's stripper in a tank top
Death Trip
The weird army sergeant and the hookers
Death Trip
No more midnights
Death Trip
I'll do anything for money
Death Trip
The cortisol runs out
Death Trip
The parking lot of Gold's Gym
Death Trip
The summer never compromises
Death Trip
They wouldn't let you into porn
Death Trip
Six-months old
Death Trip
A lifetime of food poisoning
Death Trip
Tom Selleck flashes his prick
Death Trip
She says, Death Trip
Death Trip
Put the camera to the keyhole
Death Trip
Don't say a word
Death Trip
I fucked a Gucci Mane in Tijuana
Death Trip
Took her back to the shop
Death Trip
Let's huff some gas
Death Trip

She took off her face
Death Trip
She's into smut
Death Trip
The psychic won't return my calls
Death Trip
I get visions
Death Trip
We're the only mutants left
Death Trip
Big-tittied girl in a dirty cell
Death Trip
She dressed like a scratch ticket
Death Trip
They called her the Iron Wart Hog
Death Trip

## **Don't Talk to Yourself, You're Writing**

Please note
The Theory of Unified Perversions
Has been canceled.

It's not only my fault:
It's my life's mission.

When I was born
The stars got cancer,
The sun was chemorbital,
It was so hot
I felt
Postponed,
Immaculate.

My psychic trick
Is to convince you
You want to play
A psychic trick on me.

Forgive
My inability
To sin.

A poem should be
A little piece
Of psychological warfare.

It's obvious
You don't get it.

Your backbiting society
Doesn't deserve analysis,
but here goes:

There's too many voices
Inside my head
But I don't think your voice
Is one of them.

I'm Illuminated.
That's why I always like
The plague load from the Santa Maria.

The world is a frivolous place.
Everything is already unionized
And there is no boss to fight against.

I am here only to impress
The puppets and
Their ventriloquists.

## **Twila With an Oxygen Tank**

She laughs until emptiness and nothingness are severed.

The magazine world blows apart.

In an alley she sees
Nothingness and emptiness
In perfect union.

*We are all prisoners.*
*One cage opens into the next.*
*From birth your flesh has betrayed you;*
*From birth you have desired*
*And searched.*

## **Burroughs' Last Dream**

They brought him into a clay-colored room without windows: a twin bed, a pillow and blankets all the color of the walls. He couldn't see clearly the ones who'd brought him here, nor hear their voices; they were just two gray presences communicating directly to his cerebral cortex without utterance or gesture; a warm hum behind his head that caused certain electrical pathways to open without resistance, resembling intuition while maintaining an otherness separate from his own conscious mind: commands disguised as suggestions. This device did not reciprocate: he could not see into the program or the programmer. Normally he wouldn't stand such an intrusion— maybe they'd rerouted his fear methodology—he felt subdued to the point of almost being at peace; in fact, he was sure he'd never come closer to it: a sensation much less consumptive than heroin; not oblivion: clairvoyance in the blood.

He received a message to insert himself between the sheets and go to sleep. This seemed essential. Sitting on the edge of the bed he removed his coat, vest, tie, shirt, shoes, pants and socks, then rolled back the bedding and positioned himself under the covers. In a few seconds he was asleep. A tape of consciousness played in his mind: "It's over."

He was aware of every pore in his body becoming lighter until he was weightless. He lifted off the bed. Behind his eyes he could see an image of the room with him in it. He was now six or seven feet above the bed. He wanted to go higher and as he wanted it he rose. The notion occurred to him that this ability must be under his control and that the beings who'd showed him here must be responsible for this gift, and nothing is given for free, yet he felt no apprehension; it seemed this place was governed by much more sensible laws than Man's.

The ceiling was very close now, which meant he must be seventeen or eighteen feet off the ground. He had no fear of gravity returning without notice. Sudden things didn't happen in this world. Retracting his arms back against his chest, he braced for contact with the ceiling.

Without warning his limbs dragged on him like bags of sand, his picture of the room and himself in it vanished, his eyelids refused to part: vague phosphenes impossible to focus on, behind each the mouth of obsolescence; even as he sank into them, the tape of his conscious mind remained abstracted, beyond the developing erasure. Every attempt made by his body to sit up or thrash his mind into cooperating failed. In the tape he could distinguish the punctual wheezing of the cat at his bedside and he asked if this was Death.

With the remainder of his vital force he planned to fling his right arm backwards, hoping it would generate enough momentum to jar the body awake. This would be the final go. He focused all his primacy, all his rage, into its execution: the result was a disembodied groan and a slight flinch of the right shoulder. Both mind and body found themselves exhausted and unable to ward off what would be the paramount collapse.

There was nothing left to hold on to when a sudden jolt through his spine caused his torso to snap up. His eyes were open. Maragras slunk like a beautiful white worm onto the floor and out through the open door. Moving with as much speed as an octogenerian addict can muster, the man who had always been old swiveled his legs over the side of the bed and bent down to retrieve from the nightstand a pen and the notebook Brion had given him for his 70th birthday. It was still light outside, the air in the curtains. He ran his thumb over the monogrammed "Audrey" then flipped open the cover of the journal and wrote:

*Awoke in penumbra from dream of levitation. I'd been led into a room by formless entities which I had an instinct to trust like the sheep trusts the shepherd who later butchers him. They gave me the ability to fly (float) then sucked it back. Idea for a story called* The Taxman. *Maybe it's Control telling me they have some great reward in store, all I have to do is say no more. Maybe*

*I'll take them up on the deal. What do I got to lose? Memory impressions also possibly being tampered with: my mind being used in an experiment on someone else's body?*

He closed the notebook, returning it and the pen to the nightstand, where they lay soundlessly. In a glance he scanned the room: not so much as a picture on the wall.

His thoughts turned to his work. The plot was developing around the idea of words that can drain the power of other words: when arranged correctly they gain the ability to drain the essence out of the reader. The owner of the store where these books are sold is a corpulent former Army General who sweats semen and stores the essences in a database installed in his scrotum. Every time he jacks-off a new essence seeps into his blood stream, revitalizing him, but only to a degree. In this way he thinks he's setting himself up for immortality. His voice like a worn-out reed came from nowhere and returned there without ceremony:

"Immortality: the cumulative knowledge of a species that still plays in its own shit. Of course we had to test it out on the mice initially, sir. That way you'd know we're worthy. Worthy? Worthy? Pilate? Yes, sir? Turn on the gas. But sir... Should've used it on yourselves first instead of the goddamn rats." The lab goes up in flames. The soldiers scream. "We did, sir...!"

The old man pulled his legs back onto the bed and under the sheets, waiting for the cat to re-enter the room.

## **Twila Revisited**

She's shifting
In and out of focus
Like the dew
On the hem
Of the honey locust.

## **The Cold War**

I don't know if we were spies
or just fugitives.
We were on a bus.
I was fleeing again
but confident this time
I would attain liberation,
insoluble levity,
ascent.
Everyone on the bus felt the same;
we could see ourselves gliding across the map from above
through a country of weightless gold.

Sitting next to me was an Indian girl—
Hindu, Aztec, Iroquois...
I couldn't discern her origin—
I thought she had the power to heal.

I knew I would never escape my native land,
though it seemed the journey itself was a sanctuary.

The girl asked me where I was going
and if I'd taken this route before.
I answered then asked her the same,
her eyes a window to the foot hills behind,
the desert a mask for the forest
absolved of all duration.
She had a baby in her arms.
I asked her its name.
Her lips turned ocher like herbs
and she was silent:

*This child was a gift.*
*Our destination cannot be determined.*
*Her name is October*
*and she must never awake from her dream.*

We entered a territory of wind and sand
and wheat.
This was America.

The girl pointed out the window,

*We call this place Russia*, she said.

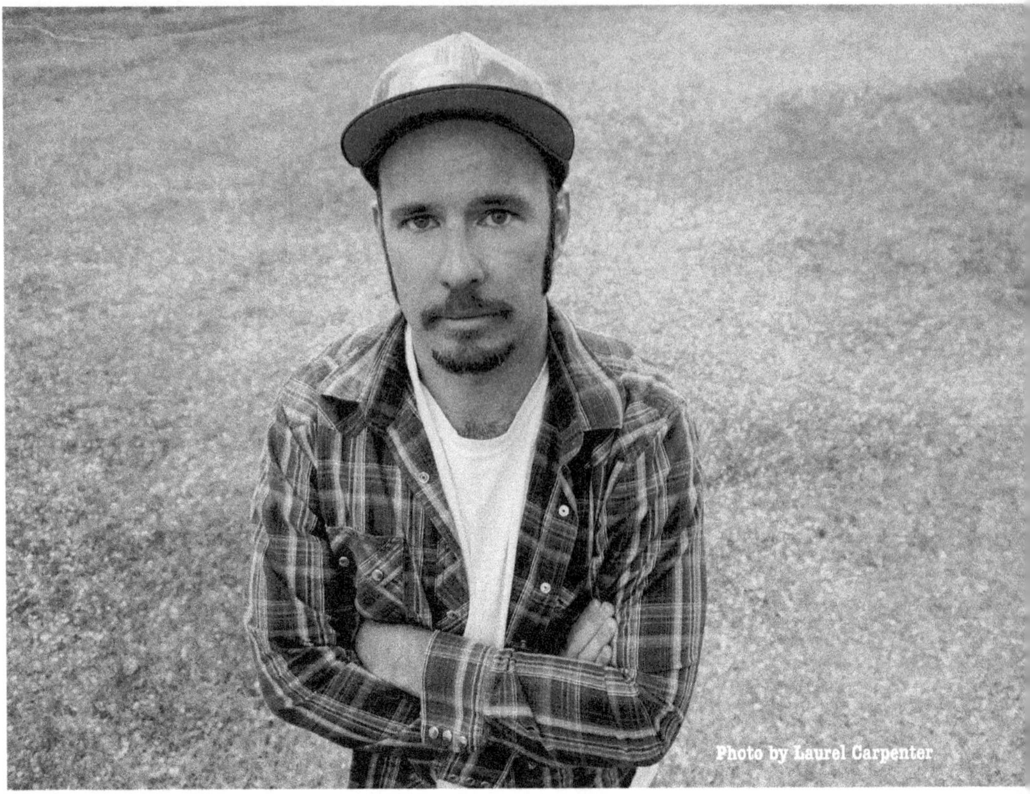

Quinten Collier is the author of the novel *Mouth, Rome* as well as the winner of the 2009 American Songwriter Lyrics Contest. He lives in Colorado.

www.ingramcontent.com/pod-product-compliance
Lightning Source LLC
Chambersburg PA
CBHW021145160426
43194CB00007B/693